"*The Happy Couple* is a guidebook that every couple should read. My wife of fifty-nine years calls marriage a struggle, and Joseph Campbell called it an ordeal. They are defining the effort that two individuals must make to create a relationship. Let the wisdom of this book help the two of you create a third entity: a true and happy relationship."

> —**Bernie Siegel, MD**, author of A Book of Miracles and The Art of Healing

"*The Happy Couple* makes a great pocket book. There will be times when you get into a bad spot with your partner and you want to do something right now to stop the stress. You only need to remember one thing: 'Where is my copy of *The Happy Couple*?' Just look up the appropriate tip and you're on your way to creating a better relationship. Plus, you can avoid another night on the couch and cold shoulders."

> —**Ellyn Bader, PhD**, founder of The Couples Institute

"When couples say they want to 'work on their relationship,' what does that really mean, and what work is required? Goldsmith's *The Happy Couple* lays it all out through clear objectives and direct behaviors. It also amply demonstrates how changed behaviors lead to changed feeling states. I can only believe that any couple who follows this set of promptings will evolve into a much better relationship."

> —**James Hollis, PhD**, Jungian analyst and author of many books, including *Hauntings: Dispelling the Ghosts Who Run Our Lives*

The Happy Couple

How to Make Happiness
a Habit One Little
Loving Thing at a Time

barton goldsmith, phd

New Harbinger Publications, Inc.

Publisher's Note

This publication is designed to provide accurate and authoritative information in regard to the subject matter covered. It is sold with the understanding that the publisher is not engaged in rendering psychological, financial, legal, or other professional services. If expert assistance or counseling is needed, the services of a competent professional should be sought.

Distributed in Canada by Raincoast Books

Copyright © 2013 by Barton Goldsmith

New Harbinger Publications, Inc.
5674 Shattuck Avenue
Oakland, CA 94609
www.newharbinger.com

Cover design by Amy Shoup
Interior design by Michele Waters-Kermes
Acquired by Melissa Kirk
Edited by Brady Kahn

Library of Congress Cataloging-in-Publication Data

Goldsmith, Barton.
  The happy couple : how to make happiness a habit one little loving thing at a time / Barton Goldsmith, PhD.
    pages cm
  ISBN 978-1-60882-872-2 (pbk. : alk. paper) -- ISBN 978-1-60882-873-9 (pdf e-book) -- ISBN 978-1-60882-874-6 (epub) 1. Marriage. 2. Interpersonal communication. 3. Man-woman relationships. I. Title.
  HQ503.G6155 2013
  306.81--dc23

                        2013037198

Printed in the United States of America

15   14   13

10   9   8   7   6   5   4   3   2   1   First printing

To my best friends,
Kathy and Piewackett.
Rest well and know that I love you.

Contents

Foreword

More than twenty-five years ago, a Unitarian minister named Robert Fulghum published a book with a simple credo: *All I Really Need to Know I Learned in Kindergarten.* The book became a best seller; its title became a cultural meme. While it was not overtly a philosophical book, it espoused a philosophy with which we could all identify: life is not really complicated. We all learned at a very early age how to live successfully with other people, but we all seem to have forgotten it as we grew older.

The same philosophy can be applied to marriage, but books on marriage tend to make it complicated. Some cloud marriage in theory with little guidance about how to actually be married; others offer advice without much theoretical basis. Some are based on science and brain research and depict the process of change as deep and complicated, requiring a steep learning curve for the couple.

However, most books on marriage agree on one thing: couples want to be happy and do not know how. And each offers its view of the perilous journey from misery to joy. For some, the reasons for a couple's unhappiness are located in the intrusion of childhood into their adult relationship, and the couple needs to achieve profound insights into their unconscious urges. Some books go to the other extreme, viewing a difficult relationship as the result of missing relationship skills; they send couples off to a sort of couples camp where they can practice. Ignorance of relationship skills is another possible cause, so couples are advised to take classes together. Pure stubbornness about their willingness to change, or "resistance," is often cited, so a stint in therapy may be considered necessary. But all couples are counseled by all marriage books that happiness is on the other side of change.

In his book *The Happy Couple*, Barton Goldsmith has done something unique. He has assembled a remarkable list of ideas and exercises for couples that, in my view, will actually work. And he has done it without the befuddlement of theory, yet every page exhibits a theory of change. Obviously, it reminded me of Fulghum's philosophy: We all learned long ago that being negative gets you nowhere. A positive attitude is a prerequisite for a good relationship. You have to make a commitment to make anything happen. Talk with your partner. Don't criticize. Have fun together. Greet each other when you come home and say goodbye when you leave. It's simple. What would make marriage work for everyone is not rocket science. Not a single suggestion or exercise is exotic or complicated or requires a college degree. All of them ring of common sense.

What I like about what Goldsmith has done is that he brings all of these "truths" together, illustrates each one with a story, and offers an exercise that would put the concept into action. What makes the book challenging to couples is that the author refuses to delude them by saying that becoming a happy couple is easy. No, but for the couple who wants the happiness they say they want, this is an amazing workbook, a map of the journey—every step of the way. The only way a couple could fail is to not do the work.

—Harville Hendrix, PhD
New York, 2013
Co-author with Helen LaKelly Hunt
of *Making Marriage Simple: Ten Truths
for Changing the Relationship You Have
into the Relationship You Want*

Acknowledgments

At New Harbinger Publications, I'd like to thank publisher Matt McKay, acquisitions editor Melissa Kirk, copyeditor Brady Kahn, and editorial manager Jess Beebe, who were all very helpful in putting this book together.

I also need to thank my editorial assistant, Sydney MacEwen, for keeping this dyslexic author on task, focused, and not too overly neurotic.

This book wouldn't exist without the readers and editors of my column, and I will be forever grateful to the *Ventura County Star* and editor Mike Blackwell and to Scripps Howard News Service and editor Bob Jones for their unwavering support, as well as to the editors of the two hundred–plus papers who have graciously run my columns.

To my loving family and lifelong friends Shelley MacEwen (Sydney's mom); Nancy, David, and Nina Padberg; Brenda and John James; Kevin Hanley;

Rebecca Love; David and Dan Richmond; Jeb, Pam, and Madison Adams; Robert Scully; Leigh Leshner; Laurie Butler; and the dearly departed Indus Arthur—thank you for your unwavering support.

I am honored to have learned from my colleagues, including Harville Hendrix, Bernie Siegel, Michael Agress, William Glasser, Judith Orloff, Gary Chapman, Linda Metzger, Jeffrey Zeig, Linda Loomis, James Hollis, Susan Shapiro Barash, Linda Gerrits, and Louise L. Hay. Some of my mentors have passed on. I acknowledge with gratitude the late Albert Ellis, David Viscott, and Elisabeth Kübler-Ross.

And, last but not at all least, there are my companion dog, Mercy, and the newest member of the household, Phoenix, a very sweet cat. There is much truth to the question "Who rescued whom?"

To my family Min, Karmyn, Kandyce, Kourtnie, and Krystal, I love you, and thank you for your inspiration.

Introduction

At some point in our lives, most of us need to deal with unsuitable habits in our relationships. They occur when we aren't paying attention to what we are doing or saying, and so we slip into a comfort zone of not being our best selves. Unfortunately, even if you don't see it, your partner is going to feel it and perhaps be hurt by your words or actions.

Bad habits can show themselves in many ways, from being disrespectful during a disagreement to neglecting to express our gratitude for the little things that our partners do for us all the time; from failing to greet our partners affectionately after a long day apart to assuming that they know what we're thinking and feeling (and becoming resentful when they don't). Bad habits can be obvious or subtle, but they all have one thing in common: they hurt your partner and they will eventually hurt your relationship.

Destructive habits can come from many places. Sometimes they come from being raised in a dysfunctional family where issues were never resolved. People learn to use defensiveness as a weapon or to try to overpower their partners, so that they don't have to take responsibility for their part of the problem. Such habits can be damaging to any relationship; if your partner is afraid to confront you with an issue, for example, nothing ever gets resolved and the hurt builds. This is painful to both of you and creates a dynamic of discomfort where the two of you are on edge most of the time.

The only way out of these patterns is to recognize them, discuss them, and make a conscious, concerted effort to change course. You need to learn how to morph hurtful habits into positive, constructive ones that will nurture the relationship.

Finding ways to alter bad habits is a necessity. Learning how to avoid hurting each other when you have a disagreement forms a bond that will allow the two of you to deal with anything life throws at you. Remember that you can disagree without being disagreeable. Learning to accentuate the positives in your relationship will help you make it the best it can be.

Although the conversation about changing your habits as a couple can be awkward, and the process may be cumbersome, it is well worth the effort. Creating new and positive habits requires catching yourself as you are engaging in a negative manner and telling yourself, *Wait, I don't have to talk or act like this. What would be a better way to communicate with my partner, so that I don't upset her?*

Even though the process seems wearisome, it actually takes only a few seconds to review what you want to say and edit the words before they come out of your mouth. The same goes for actions that your mate may find inappropriate. Think before you act.

By repeating good habits over and over, you will create a new way of being, and you and your partner will be grateful that you did. Trusting that you can change your old patterns is part of the cure. Part of this you can do on your own. Part of it you can do together with your partner. The decision to do it is up to you.

How to Use This Book

This book explains in a straightforward manner how you can achieve a more positive relationship with your partner, overcome difficulties, and develop not only deeper communication but a deeper emotional connection—all of which leads to having more fun together and a healthier sex life. In each chapter, you will find practical advice and exercises to help you break the bad habits that are getting in the way.

Start by finding a chapter that deals with an issue you're having in your relationship right now. If the content of the chapter is helpful, share it with your partner. Next, talk about the bad habit that you want to confront, commit to making a change, and then act on it by doing an exercise or following up on a suggestion from the chapter you just read.

You can then start reading the book from the beginning or choose another chapter that speaks to something you're facing at the moment. Most importantly, quickly share with your partner any new insights gained while reading. I designed this book to help you keep your relationship on a positive track. The idea was to make the process as simple and as easy as possible. Reading and talking about each chapter doesn't have to take a long time. You can take as long as you wish, but don't spend hours on one issue. Spending too much time on one thing can wear a relationship down. Start slowly for now and, if you're so moved, work your way up to an hour of discussion once a week. That's all most couples need.

After you've experienced some success with a new way of communicating or being together, making it a habit in your relationship will be less intimidating. A number of couples I know choose to talk about their relationships during evening walks or while bike riding. This casual approach can work well, because you can release some of your emotional anxiety through physical exercise.

So congratulate yourself and your partner. You are about to move your relationship forward and create a safer and more loving space in your life. Trust your own process, and if you get lost or confused, remember that you will always be able to find your way through your life's issues by looking within yourself. All it takes is patience and persistence.

1 *Communication*

What do you think is the most important part of a relationship? Trust, intimacy, or perhaps love? All three are valuable, and you can't have a relationship without them, but they are not the most important part. That would be communication. A relationship cannot thrive or even survive without good communication.

Good communication is not about never arguing. It's not about being able to read each other's minds or about being able to have long discussions on a variety of topics. It is about being able to share all the emotional, mental, physical, and spiritual aspects of your life, without being judged or feeling devalued. It is about you and your partner talking intimately about feelings and missteps that occur on a daily basis. And it is about wanting to share your life with another human being who isn't psychic and needs to hear your words to be able to understand and properly care for you.

Many people think that their mates should already know what is going on inside their heads and hearts before anything is said. Unfortunately, all the good psychics are busy with their websites or giving tarot card readings to Jerry Springer, and you cannot expect your partner to read your mind. You must be able to say what's going on for you in a way that your partner will understand. You can use some basic communication steps in a variety of situations.

exercise: Communicating with Your Partner

Step 1. If you sense something is bothering your partner—regarding work, family, your relationship, or any other area—ask if he'd like to talk about it with you. If he is not ready to talk at the moment, don't worry. Tell him you will be there for him when he is.

Step 2. Conversely, if anything is bothering you, ask your partner for a conversation if you need it, but make sure he is in a receptive place. You can easily do that by asking, "Is this a good time to talk?"

Step 3. Be sure to listen very carefully to what is said, and say everything you have to say very carefully. Respond to your partner's needs, or be clear about what he needs to do to respond to yours.

Step 4. If you feel there may be more to say, ask that the topic be left open. Once you feel the problem is resolved, say so.

Step 5. Continue to discuss this topic every day until both of you feel that you've resolved it.

It helps to learn how to ask clarifying questions. For example, if your partner is down in the dumps, rather than taking it personally, you could ask how he is feeling and if there is anything you could do to help. Being proactive, rather than letting the one you care for sit in his own pain, is a great way to show your love, and it's a wonderful communication tool.

Asking clarifying questions will help you develop solutions. When your loved one comes to you with a problem, dig a little deeper to get a well-rounded picture of what's going on, so that you can give your best advice. By listening, you'll help your partner mellow out from the stress of what's bothering him. It also saves you from wasting all those days you used to spend not talking.

When there is silence in a relationship, it is not necessarily golden. In fact, it may be hurting you. Not enough communication can make people feel disconnected; they simply drift away emotionally from their relationships and their partners. Everybody needs to feel heard and to have someone to talk to.

Even if you think you have nothing to talk about, you can always find something to discuss. Family, friends, and finances are just three places to start. Most people like complaining a little, so you can always ask your partner what his feelings are about politics or the state of the world. If he shows little interest, don't give up. Explain the need for communication and, without being a nag, keep bringing up little questions that need little answers, and before you know it, you will be having actual conversations.

If neither of you is a big talker, developing the habit of communicating may require a little more effort. If you are starting from scratch, begin by having at least one meal a day together where you talk for at least thirty minutes about what you did that day or what you are planning to do. You can discuss family issues if there are any. By sitting down and talking as you share a meal together, you can take your time to think about what it is you need to say. This takes the stress out of trying to have a conversation just for the sake of conversation. Once you get used to talking over a meal, communicating will become much easier. You'll find yourself in a more harmonious relationship, with fewer disagreements, as the two of you get used to discussing what's on your minds.

Good communication is not only about your words (although when you are communicating electronically or by telephone, words become more important). It is also about your tone and about eye contact. You will get much more from any conversation if you look at the person with whom you are talking. Trying to have a conversation while you are in different rooms is like trying to make love in separate beds: it doesn't work.

Because so much of our communication today is electronic, I recommend texting or e-mailing during the workday, if you can't talk. This is something you have to get good at. Sure, it's fine to send a quick text about picking up something or confirming times. However, conveying emotion may take a little more than a smiley face or other emoticon. Do your best to put some heart into your keyboard communications. Use words of love and support. It doesn't have to happen every time, but it does need to happen every day.

Communication is important in our relationships because it is the one true way that couples can convey emotions and states of mind. Remember, you shouldn't assume you know how your partner feels; you have to ask in order to confirm your suspicions. By asking, you will make your partner feel cared for and validated. We all need to know that there is someone in our lives who cares about how we feel. Dealing with difficult feelings is so much easier when you can talk about them to that person who is your other half. It's part of what makes the two of you a whole.

Having good communication on a regular basis may be even more important than having good sex. When you ask older couples in successful long-term relationships what their secret is, they will tell you that it's good communication. When someone you love is willing to listen to you about whatever it is you have to say, the feeling you get is simply life affirming.

The positive effect that good communication has on relationships can be amazing. It can take relationships that are broken and fix them, and it can do the same for hearts. Good communication skills will serve you for the rest of your life and will make your days together better than ever.

2 Gratitude

Do you ever feel truly grateful for the partner you have and for your relationship? Would you like to show your gratitude in better and more potent ways? Has there ever been a time when you or your partner should have expressed his or her gratitude but didn't?

One reason I love the Thanksgiving holiday is that it reminds us all that we need to be grateful for what we have. Certainly, the Pilgrims didn't have much. Mostly they had hardships, but they still believed in expressing gratitude for what good they did have.

What eludes most of us is how to make this feeling a part of our daily lives so that it's reflected in our behaviors, especially toward those we love. Unfortunately, even if our lives aren't always what we think they should be, we can easily forget that we need to be thankful for what we have.

You can't bargain with gratitude. For example, it doesn't work to tell yourself, *I'll be grateful when I get this deal done or when she says she loves me.* If gratitude isn't a constant in your mental universe, then you may be pushing away some of what you want or be making someone you love feel unappreciated. Others sense our attitudes even if we don't say anything.

If you are confused about what this habit of gratitude is, think of it as a deep-seated appreciation for something you have (whether earned or received as a gift) that could reasonably be gone tomorrow.

exercise: Being Thankful Every Day

To build the habit of gratitude, wake up every day thankful for your life and basic health. Offer your thanks out loud or repeat it silently to yourself. You can keep it simple, such as "I am grateful for my life and basic health," or use your own words to make your expression of thanks more personal. Repeat this blessing daily. Try doing it every day for a week. This is a great way to get a feel for what it means to be grateful. You can then take in and be thankful for more complex aspects of your life, like a loving relationship, an understanding partner, and the other people and things in your life that make you happy.

Giving thanks should be a daily ritual, because giving thanks reinforces the good that has come to us and allows us to let go of negative feelings that we no longer need to hold on to.

Creating the habit of gratitude is something that will serve you in all areas of your life. Those who are grateful have fewer resentments and are usually happier people, and the benefits can even extend to your physical well-being. Nothing says "I love you" to your partner more than being grateful that she is in your life. Having an attitude of gratitude tells the one you love that you appreciate and respect her. This attitude gets communicated in all that you do with and for each other. It has more to do with creating happiness than most people think.

If you are hurt and angry, it is hard to find the gratitude within. You have to get beyond what is going on for you in the moment and seek some peace by remembering the things for which you are grateful.

One way to fight depression and increase your happiness quotient is to keep a gratitude journal. Doing this exercise as a couple can change the way both of you feel, as you put pen to paper to confirm and reinforce your positive feelings.

exercise: Keeping a Gratitude Journal

Step 1. Get a couple of blank books (one for each of you), or some blank paper, and place them on your nightstand. Then, before you go to bed, take a few minutes to identify some things you are grateful for and write down three to five of these things.

Step 2. Come up with new ideas every evening. Do this on a nightly basis for at least two weeks, and you will start to notice changes in how you look at and feel about life and your relationship.

Step 3. At an appropriate time, show what you've written to the one you love. This is a great way to share your deepest feelings for your relationship. If you are grateful for your partner's presence in your life and grateful for her qualities and actions, you need to let her know it. Communicating your gratitude will bring the two of you closer together.

Step 4. Make a separate list of all the things in your relationship for which you feel grateful. This will become a reminder of all you have going for you.

One of life's most powerful moments may be when you hear your loved one tell you how grateful she is for your energy. The positive emotions flow through you like a warm drink filling your heart. To know that you have done something for the person you love—and that it made her life better—is affirming on so many levels. The validation that you receive is amazing. When your loved one acknowledges your positive actions, it inspires you to do more for her. And knowing that your mate really, really likes that you are together gives your relationship an extra boost.

Gratitude is the glue that holds couples together when things get tough. It moves both of you to a higher level where you can see what it is that really matters. Being grateful for this life together makes it so much sweeter than if you were complaining about everything.

If the truth is that you are both better off and have more love than when you first got together, that's something to be grateful for. If it isn't your truth yet, it is something you need to work on.

The first step is to recognize and honor what it is that you are grateful for in your relationship. If you can imagine your life without the one you love, and allow yourself to feel that emptiness for one second, you will know what I'm saying. The strength of your love, and having her hand to hold while you walk through this world together, is one of life's greatest gifts.

Keeping a gratitude journal is one way to share your gratitude with each other. Another way is to sit down together and tell each other how grateful you are to be in each other's lives and how you want to keep going and growing as a team. We so seldom take the time to do it, yet this simple exercise is extremely powerful and can leave you feeling wonderful. Try it.

Another way to show your gratitude is to remember to say "thank you" for those little things we all come to expect. Whether it's for brewing the morning coffee or offering a back rub at night, thanking each other is going to keep you both feeling appreciated.

Of course, sometimes actions can be more powerful than words. You can show your gratitude with a warm and loving hug, a flower from the garden placed on her desk, or a little note left on the kitchen table that says, "Thanks for being with me."

Much of the time, our feelings of discontentment come from fearing that we are losing what we have or not getting what we want. We fail to appreciate where we are in life at the moment. A habit of gratitude will help you see that what you have is better than whatever it is you may think you want.

3 Humor

Could your relationship use a good dose of healthy humor? Have you ever said something to your partner that you thought was really funny, but he didn't "get it"? Do you or your mate sometimes engage in humor that causes someone's feelings to get hurt?

Having humor in a relationship is important. Life cannot be serious all the time. You have to make room for a little lightheartedness to have a balanced love life. If your time together tends to be serious, please know that injecting a little humor into your relationship will not be difficult and can only do you good.

Cultivating a habit of humor requires that you be respectful in your banter. This is not stand-up comedy or razor-sharp repartee. It is two people playing with words and with each other. Keep it harmless and blameless, and never use humor as a weapon. Once you clarify those ground rules, it will be easier to have more fun with each other.

If your partner sometimes makes jokes that you don't like or understand, remember that this doesn't make him a bad person. He's probably only trying to lighten things up a bit. And if you don't go with it, you are likely to bump heads, and one of you might get upset. Sometimes when we are in serious frames of mind, we easily can get offended. But if your sweetheart's jokes are neither biting nor aimed at you in particular, you need to make room for him to say things that he finds funny, even if you are unable to find the humor in it all the time. Again, this is different if you become the butt of your mate's jokes, but if he is just trying to have some fun, more good is being done than harm.

I find that humor, used wisely, can help defuse many uncomfortable situations. Having a sense of humor is so important that there is an annual psychologists' conference devoted to how to use humor in therapy. If it can make a difference there, it can make a difference in your relationship.

If your partner's humor does offend you at times, it is perfectly fine to have a conversation about it and set some appropriate boundaries. Some folks enjoy insult or put-down humor, and that won't work in a relationship. Your jokes and actions should be life enhancing, and they should never make things worse. So if your partner's humor is sometimes hurtful rather than funny, you may want to have a discussion about how to keep humor on the right track.

exercise: Keeping Humor on the Right Track

Step 1. Ask your partner to have a talk with you and, even though it is a serious subject, at least ask in a soft and light manner. There is no need to get (or make your partner) defensive. Remember, this should be a healing talk with an eye on the future.

Step 2. Explain why the type of humor your partner uses sometimes hurts you, and be prepared with an example: "When you said _____, I felt devalued and cheap." Be sure to use an *I-message*, in which you explain how you felt. When you share your true feelings, your partner will realize that he has been insensitive. Once he recognizes this behavior, it is a simple choice to change it.

Step 3. Ask your partner how he would feel if that type of humor were directed at him, and give him a moment to think before responding. This is where your partner will feel your pain and be able to take it in. Once he feels how you feel, he will have a much better understanding of how he needs to change his jokes.

Step 4. Brainstorm to find a solution, such as using a different style of humor or avoiding teasing. Neither of you wants to have your fun become hurtful, so setting appropriate boundaries is a necessary step.

Creating a positive habit of humor in your relationship will give your relationship a new depth. Even if you don't think you're very funny, you can approach your life and love with a fine sense of humor. It's not about making jokes that rival Jerry Seinfeld's. It's about seeing the lighter side of life and reveling in it. Life can be ironic, which can be both fun and funny. Once you get started, it's not hard to find the humor in a conversation or action and to appreciate your mate's sense of humor, in turn. Many couples find that laughing together helps to release tension, and it's a bonding experience. Here are some ideas for how to laugh together more often.

- Watch funny shows. One way to add humor to your love life is to watch sitcoms together or go to films that are funny. Better to watch a show that makes you smile than to watch one that makes you cry. There is a reason why all the major broadcast networks have comedians on their late-night schedule. Comedy clubs work too.

- Make a home movie. The two of you may enjoy hamming it up in front of the camera, so get out the old camcorder or use your digital camera or smartphone, and be humorous with each other. Then watch your antics together.

- Go on a vacation. Seeing the lighter side of life can be easier while vacationing, because everybody tends to feel happy and at ease. Vacationing together should be fun, but if you look at it as an adventure in chaos, you will lose your ability to see and enjoy the humor in it. Better to appreciate the humor in the chaos and enjoy yourself from the moment you start planning. If you are going to take a vacation and not have any laughs, you might as well stay at home.

- Wash the dishes. Seeing the lighter side of life is not just about saying funny things. It's also about doing things together with a sense of humor. You can use humor to break up the monotony of household chores. I know couples who crack each other up so much that it can take them hours to do the dishes, they are having so much fun together.

A sure sign of a healthy relationship is when you are facing a difficult situation together and you both can see the humor in it. You know that no matter what you are confronting, you will get through it together and be able to smile (at times) through the process.

We cannot travel through life without hitting a few speed bumps. When you can locate the humor in it, life will be much easier. Sometimes that may take a little effort, and perhaps you will see something as amusing and your partner will not, or the other way around. Whatever the case, follow the joy and try to deal lightly with whatever life throws at you. A sense of humor may be the best friend you can have (next to your mate) when the world isn't working exactly the way you would like.

Laughing together can only help your relationship. Nothing says "I love you" more than laughing at your partner's bad jokes, especially if you've heard them a hundred times before. And there may be nothing more wonderful than making your sweetheart laugh.

Laughter keeps you in touch with the bright side of life (which isn't always easy), and it creates brain chemicals that make you feel good about yourself and make it easier for you to give and receive love. Creating the habit of humor is a gift. Open it together.

4 *Acknowledgment*

When was the last time you acknowledged your partner by saying "I love you" or by telling her how grateful you are to have her in your life? How do you feel when your partner leaves for the day without saying good-bye? What if you've had a misunderstanding and one of you refuses to make an apology, even though no one disagrees about who was wrong? Acknowledging our partners and our mistakes is a positive habit that we all need to create in our relationships.

Acknowledgment can take many forms, but a proper acknowledgment is any statement or action that conveys your positive feelings about something your partner has said or done. Letting your partner know that you are grateful for her actions and being supportive of her efforts will make her feel better about herself and better about you and your relationship. It is a very easy thing, and I suggest you look for opportunities to show the one you love that you are receiving her positive energy and responding appropriately.

- Remember to say good-bye. Greetings and farewells are important in a relationship because they acknowledge a shift in your togetherness. Acknowledging that you will not see your partner for the rest of the day, as she leaves in the morning, changes how both of you will deal with the time you have to spend apart. When your partner leaves you with an extra dose of love, it can help you make it through the difficulties of the day. If a gap exists, and you start to wonder how your relationship is going, because you left each other in silence that day, it will make the day more difficult to get through. Make saying good-bye to your partner the last thing you do before you head out the door in the morning—this habit will ensure that the two of you start the day on the right foot.

- Greet each other with a ten-second hug and kiss. Heartwarming greetings can be very easy to practice regularly. If you've been apart, give your mate a ten-second hug and kiss to really let her know you are connected. She will feel it, and her emotional high will return to you instantly.

The bond you will feel is very real and is one of those things that makes life worth living.

- Express your thanks. Acknowledge your partner whenever she does something nice for you. You'd be surprised at how good your saying "thank you" can make her feel. It will inspire her to continue doing things that warrant that kind of response. Proper acknowledgment makes you want to do things that let your partner know how much you care. When your mate does something nice for you, a failure to acknowledge it with a "thank you" can be taken as being rude. The manners you were taught as a kid are even more important when you become an adult and are in a loving relationship. If your partner feels unappreciated, she won't be as emotionally (or physically) available as you might like.

- Express your appreciation on a deeper level. Besides saying "thank you," you can say how much you appreciate what your partner does for you all the time and how grateful you are to have her in your life. Doing this will make her feel valued at the highest level. Looking into her eyes as you are talking will help get the message across.

- Say "I love you." Saying "I love you" costs you nothing and pays big dividends. When you are comfortable in your love, and your connection is acknowledged, it makes you feel that you are with the right person and that life is fulfilling. Hearing the words will remove any doubt and make your road easier to navigate.

- Give your partner credit. Giving your partner credit whenever possible for things she's accomplished, from doing the dishes to doing the taxes, is always worthwhile. Saying "well done" in any way, shape, or form is a habit that will enhance your dynamic as a couple. It's important to acknowledge how your partner makes life easier for you by doing all the little things that she does. Acknowledging each other in this way empowers you to take on the rest of the world together.

Receiving these types of acknowledgment fills your emotional bank account and gives you strength. When that account is overdrawn and you feel emotionally bankrupt, your partner may need to make a deposit by giving you the emotional support you require. But don't expect her to be a mind reader. You have to find ways of communicating with your partner when you feel emotionally drained and are in need of greater support.

One of the best ways to do this is to ask if she has a moment to sit down with you and chat. Then you can share whatever it is that's making you feel emotionally depleted. Knowing that someone is really listening will help you refuel. Getting out the negativity will make room for positive, reinforcing feelings to come in.

You also need to ask for what you need. If you feel like you need to be held closely or you need to hear some supportive and endearing words, learn to ask for it. You may feel that if you have to ask, you are diluting the power of what you are going to receive, but if you don't ask, you may well not get any of your needs met.

Apologizing is another important form of acknowledgment. When you love someone and you accidentally hurt her feelings, the only appropriate response is to say, "I'm sorry, it won't happen again," and to make clear to your partner that you understand how your actions made her feel. Doing this is simple, takes very little energy, and will heal the wound that your loved one is feeling, so why hold back?

There are many reasons why people refuse to apologize, but most of the time it comes down to stubbornness and being unwilling to admit having made an error. If this is true for you, get over it. Apologizing is not a sign of weakness. On the contrary, making a heartfelt apology is a sign of strength, because it shows your ability to let go of things and feelings that no one feels good about holding on to. Your apologies should be sincere and complete.

exercise: Learning How to Say You're Sorry

Step 1. Take some time to figure out what you're sorry about and why.

Step 2. Be clear about what you are apologizing for, so that your apology is pure and without any ulterior motives like getting your way, or ending a fight just for the sake of ending it.

Step 3. Sit down in a relaxed setting with your partner and voice your apology in clear, simple language.

Step 4. Ask if there's anything else that's still bothering your partner and that you may not have acknowledged in your apology. This will help to resolve any remaining issues.

Step 5. Ask if there is anything you can do to make up for what happened.

Step 6. Promise that it won't happen again.

Whether it's saying you're sorry or expressing how glad you are to have each other in your lives, acknowledgment stabilizes your partner and makes your relationship closer. Without it, your partner will wonder if she is where she belongs. When there is very little or no positive emotional support coming from our partners, we begin to question our relationships and then ourselves. If you are never told that you are good enough, you may start to believe that you're not, and this changes how you view and relate to others. You can end up feeling poorly about yourself, which will have a negative impact on your relationship.

This is why the habit of acknowledgment is so important. When both of you feel good about who you are and who you are with, and you regularly convey these positive feelings to each other, the dynamic of your relationship is going to be more positive, no question. A wonderful feeling of togetherness can come simply from acknowledgement.

Once acknowledging each other becomes a regular habit, you will have fewer arguments, you will accomplish more, and you'll feel warmer toward each other. The payoff for developing the habit of acknowledgment is huge. Remember that good habits are developed by repeating the appropriate actions and behaviors a few dozen times in a row. Be proactive and let the one you love know that you appreciate her.

5 Interdependence

Do you ever notice couples who seem so deeply connected to each other that you can't tell where one person ends and the other begins? Do you also notice couples who seem to be so distant from each other that you are surprised they are together?

We all relate to one another in different ways. Some people are very independent in relationships, others are dependent on their partners, and a number of people are codependent (they put aside their own well-being to maintain their relationships).

Being truly interdependent is the healthiest way we can interact with those close to us. This is where two people, both strong individuals, are involved with each other in a supportive manner, without sacrificing themselves or compromising their values. What they have is a balanced relationship. When two people each have lives of their own and they come together out of a mutual choice to share those lives, then a lot of learning and growth can take place. There needs to be a nice balance of space and joining to really flourish. Having this kind of relationship is possible with just a little awareness and understanding.

First, you need to assess where you are right now. You may feel that your partner is way too independent and doesn't want to be with you often enough. Without balance, your relationship will always feel out of sync, which isn't a great formula for a harmonious adult connection. Likewise, if there is too much neediness, or so much dependency that there's no life outside of the relationship, then there will be no growth. Instead, you will have stagnation.

When one partner is very needy, it can push a relationship into a parent-child type of dynamic. Needy partners can't seem to do anything without their mates, and a partner being unavailable can create arguments and resentment. This can easily be a relationship breaker, and if either you or your partner is too dependent, you will need to initiate some changes before too much damage has occurred. First, you will need to talk together about reversing any dependency that exists in your relationship. This isn't about blaming or shaming. If your partner is too dependent, it's about helping him see his own world in a way that isn't threatening. Since you are a large part of that world, you need to look at how you can be there for your partner but without fostering dependency.

Reading chapter 21 together will help both of you learn how to be more secure in your relationship. Remember to remind each other that no one is going anywhere, and no big changes are in the works. Let your partner know that you are dedicated to the relationship, and take your time to allow the words to soak in. This will help to ease any insecurities or doubts, which tend to be the roots of dependency. When both of you feel secure in your relationship, you have the foundation for true interdependence.

You also need to watch out for too much independence, which will bring about its own set of difficulties. There has to be the understanding that you got into this so that you could be a couple. If one of you is off doing your own thing for days on end, your mate will wonder why he is in the relationship in the first place.

If you feel there is too much independence in your relationship, gently bring up the topic as something you want to discuss and change. If you feel that your mate is unavailable, you need to have a serious discussion about your feelings. But do it with kindness and consideration. If the discussion makes your partner feel bad, it will be much harder to reach a viable resolution.

Coming up with some suggestions for how to change your dynamic will help to get the ball rolling, and your partner will be less likely to feel defensive or feel like he has to scramble to come up with something to add to the conversation. For example, getting closer could be as simple as exchanging a couple of phone calls or even texting during the day. You may need more nurturing (see chapter 13), or perhaps your mate has let his work take over his life. Once you know where the problem lies, you will easily see where you can make changes to repair it.

exercise: Creating Interdependence

Step 1. Sit down with each other and take a good look at where you are in your relationship.

Step 2. Give each other credit for the positive ways in which you help keep the relationship balanced.

Step 3. Talk about how dependency or too much independence may be affecting your relationship's well-being, and ask your partner to do the same. If you have issues, be honest and tender as you state your feelings, and use I-messages. Remember to cite examples.

Step 4. Once you have established where you are, begin looking at how you got here. Can you pinpoint when certain unhelpful patterns first developed? Ask each other some questions like "Where did we go off track?" or "Is this what you really want?"

Step 5. Once you have processed where you are, ask each other, "How can we make it better for both of us?"

Having this conversation will help to clarify how you each participate in keeping your relationship on or off track and how you can create greater interdependence. Getting clarity before embarking on a journey of change is imperative. Before doing this exercise with your partner, create some of your own questions that are specific to your relationship and lifestyle. If one of you travels, the two of you will have different issues from couples who are around each other 24/7.

Interdependence means having time to yourself as well as time together, so make sure you have enough time to yourself. If your mate won't let you have any alone time, you need to bring up this problem and discuss it gently. There is no crime in asking for personal time. We all need it now and then. Every relationship is different, and there are myriad possibilities for making things better if you both want to.

Your relationship may seem so far from the interdependent model that having this kind of interchange is hard to imagine. The truth is that it's never too late to have a great relationship. All the two of you have to do is make the commitment and do the work involved. Most of the time it isn't hard; it just requires patience, practice, and forgiveness.

The best motivation for this is to realize that when your other half feels good about your relationship, you will feel good about it too. Be aware that you're making these changes not only for your partner, or for your relationship, but also for yourself. And that isn't selfish. It's appropriate, and it's part of what makes interdependence a laudable goal for your relationship.

If you don't take time for yourself, you won't be as good a partner. The same is true if you take too much time apart from the one you love. You need to find ways to balance time together and time apart so that being together is something that you both look forward to wholeheartedly.

- Give your partner a night out. A great way to support your partner is to encourage him to spend an evening out with friends (if you have kids, this also means you're on child-care duty). Time spent with close friends is different from time spent with a significant other. Both kinds of time are healthy and necessary for maintaining balance in your romantic relationship.

- Encourage each other to pursue different interests. While it's important to make time to do things together, it's also normal and healthy to pursue different interests. You should pursue your own hobbies or interests even if they don't involve your partner, and you should encourage your partner to do the same. Spending time away from your partner doing things that interest you will give you something to talk about later when you're together again, and sharing what you each did can be a lot of fun.

- Enjoy doing activities apart but in the same room. Doing something different from what your partner is doing, even when in the same room, is another way of creating balance. One of you can listen to music with headphones on while the other reads a good book. Doing different things in the same place gives you some independence and togetherness at the same time.

There are many other ways to foster the habit of interdependence. Your goal should be to figure out what works best for both of you. Again, the key to interdependence is to give each other balanced time and energy. Establishing a habit of interdependence is a great way to ensure that your relationship will have what it needs to grow and bloom. It will give both of you what you need to keep your relationship balanced.

People can live in unbalanced relationships for a lifetime. What many often don't see is that by making some simple changes in how we relate to our partners, we can change our lives for the better. Living in an interdependent relationship, you each will receive nurturing and respect. What a nice way to go through life.

6 *Celebration*

Do you celebrate the good things in your relationship? Are your celebrations limited to special events like birthdays and the holidays? Do you want more affirmation of important days and the specialness of your relationship?

When the love you feel makes you want to dance like nobody's watching, you have cause to celebrate. That special feeling is rare, and having it in your heart is quite an amazing gift. It makes you feel like wrapping your arms around your love and never letting go. Yes, this is love and it should be celebrated.

Most couples enjoy outings of various kinds, but oftentimes they are not celebrations. When we get into the habit of celebrating more, it lends additional energy to our relationships. Just having a successful (not necessarily perfect) relationship is cause for celebration, and celebrating it provides you with a deeper sense of what your love is all about.

Every day can't be a celebration, but you can always celebrate parts of the day, or even certain moments and actions. Having a celebratory attitude means that you look for the positive, and when you find it, you say something affirmative about it to your partner, and you smile together. It's that simple, and it will change the way you think and feel.

The more you are able to acknowledge the good things in your life, the stronger they will become, which will lead to greater happiness in your relationship and beyond. And celebrating often can have a significant impact on how you deal with difficulties. Whatever is going on becomes easier because you have a memory bank filled with good things that have happened and that you've celebrated together.

Creating a celebration can seem a little daunting or over-the-top for some people. But when you begin to understand the positive emotional power you receive from this habit, you will want it to become more a part of your life than ever before.

Celebrations can take many forms. Celebrating over the fact that you just got a rebate check in the mail is different from celebrating over the fact that you have a good relationship. Some events are best served a high five, and others deserve a candlelit dinner, but the ways you can celebrate are endless.

Throwing a big anniversary party is one way to celebrate; simply telling your partner how much you love her is another. Little gestures go a long way. How would it make you feel to reach into your pocket and find a note from your partner saying "I love you—let's celebrate!" That has got to make your day (and perhaps your night as well).

You should always acknowledge your successes, even small ones, with a celebration of some kind. Celebrating success often comes naturally, whereas celebrating your love may happen less often; but you can celebrate your successes and your love for each other at the same time. When you have a success in life or work, the truth is that your partner was part of it, so you now have yet another reason to feel like celebrating.

Sometimes you may feel ambivalent about celebrating a particular achievement that deserves a celebration. For instance, if your partner gets a promotion—and a raise—that she's really been wanting, it may mean that she will be spending less time at home in the evenings. Celebrating in this case may be a bit more challenging because you have mixed emotions. If you find it difficult to embrace your partner's success, however, it's a sign that you need to work through the issue, within yourself and with your partner. Be careful not to dismiss your mate's victory or taint it in any way. Give her the praise she deserves and help her honor getting something she wanted for both of you.

Another scenario that can stir up mixed feelings is when one partner loses weight and gets into shape, and the other doesn't. This is a challenging situation for anybody. If you were the one who lost weight, your partner may well have been on your team while you are thinking about or actually in the process of getting fit. But once you hit your goal, it may have brought up feelings of insecurity in the one you love. When she sees you looking more attractive, she may feel insecure about your whether or not you want to stay with her. She may fear that you will attract or be attracted to other women.

The answer here is not only to celebrate your success, but to discuss the situation and come to terms with it, so both of you feel good about the achievement. Don't let talking about it take away from the joy, but make sure that there is a solid understanding between the two of you. If one of you got a job promotion and it will mean more time away from home, discuss how to create some balance in this situation to give you the quality time and quality of life that every couple needs. If one of you has been working out and gotten into great shape, talk about any insecurities that come up for the other partner; it's a natural part of the growth process. It's wise not to come to this with an attitude, or it will be difficult to get any positive feelings out of your discussion. Look at what it is that you are gaining and what it is that you have to give up. In most cases, it is worth the effort to look closely, because over time, things change, and as your mate gets better at what she does and at being who she is, she will most likely have more time and energy for you.

When you sit down together and actually discuss what it is you have to celebrate and any other feelings that may come up, it makes you as a closer couple. Looking at the good as well as the confounding and sharing your thoughts with each other is a bonding experience, and that is another reason why this habit is important to develop. Celebrating your relationship is easier when you remember a few important facts:

- Being in a relationship is good for you. Married people tend to live longer than their unmarried counterparts. They also tend to have higher happiness levels. Of course, there is no crime in being single. Some people prefer being single and feel happier that way, and it may be your destiny. However, marriage does seem to make sense from a health standpoint.

- Those who continue to create more love in their lives create more opportunity, money, and fun.

When you have someone by your side who is striving for the same goals, you will reach them much more easily.

- Relationships can help to make us better people. Often we have the energy to do things for others that we wouldn't do for ourselves. Love is powerful in that way. If your partner brings out the best in you, she is a keeper.

- You can get more done with a partner. Sometimes it's a motivation thing. Other times, it's just nice to have company, but whatever the reason, four hands can get more done than two. Putting your heads and hearts together helps, too.

Keeping these reminders in the forefront of your mind creates a pattern for the rest of your relationship. Feeling love in your life makes the bad stuff less bad, and celebrating your relationship is a great way to increase your level of satisfaction with your partner.

So the next time something good happens, don't just say, "That's cool." Do something to celebrate it with the person who helped you make it happen. Your love life will be better off for it.

7 Playfulness

Do you wish that your relationship could be a little more fun? Do you feel that you can't find the time to play with your partner?

My other half and I have ways of connecting that I think could help make any couple feel closer to each other, so I'll share a few of them.

Where's the bear? For Valentine's Day, my loving partner gave me a little bear holding a rose. I'm not a big stuffed-animal fan. The thought of half a dozen bears resting comfortably on my pillows just seems unmanly, but I accepted the gift in the loving spirit it was given, figuring it would probably end up as a dog toy in the near future. Since then, the little bear has shown up in a number of different places—in the bathroom (sitting on the throne), on my desk pretending to write my books, next to the front door to greet me when my partner has been unable to—and it does give me a little lift. This game is something I seldom think about, but whenever the bear resurfaces, I always smile, and it inspires me to reciprocate in some way.

Card exchange. Whenever one of us gives the other a card, it is never in its original form. We add words to the ones that are already there, draw silly pictures, or enclose something meaningful (my favorite is some rose petals). We never just sign our names. We always add appropriate sentiments. It really makes what can be a perfunctory action a truly loving gesture. We also write each other little love notes. Putting energy into the written word is more moving than a text or an e-mail. Whether handwritten on a heart-shaped piece of paper or your letterhead, the impact is potent, and it is something you'll save to rediscover and smile at again sometime down the road. I especially love it when I find something in my briefcase; she likes finding notes on her pillow. Mailing a card or note is also a wonderful gesture. People rarely do that anymore, so it has greater meaning.

Our month-a-versary. On the twelfth of every month, we celebrate the day we met. Sometimes the celebration is small, such as dinner at home, and sometimes it is spectacular, like a night on the town. The activity is less important than simply knowing that, no matter what, we have a day that is special to us at least once a month.

Savoring memories. Something we have in common that strengthens our bond is that we both like to take pictures—lots of pictures. I'm happy printing one or two and putting them in the family gallery; my partner likes to create scrapbooks, including ticket stubs, programs, notes, and the like. Upon occasion, we go through the scrapbooks and pictures on the computer. Never once has this activity done anything except make us feel closer to each other.

Feel free to borrow any of these ideas, or find your own ways of playfully recognizing your relationship and making each other feel special. Discovering things that make both of you smile is a relationship builder.

Playfulness benefits a relationship, and even little actions that might seem silly or trivial have a much deeper meaning in the big picture. There is thoughtfulness, caring, love, and fun all mixed together, which serves to strengthen the foundation of your connection.

It doesn't take a lot of effort to keep your love growing. Every time you do something to make your partner smile, it creates chemicals like oxytocin, sometimes called "the cuddle hormone," in both of your brains, which makes you feel closer to each other. Connecting at a deeper level is a benefit of playing with your partner.

Being playful and happy-go-lucky, at least some of the time is healthy and necessary and rather than always focusing on really deep and serious emotions (even if they're good ones), you have to take some time to play with each other. However, we need to remember that if we're feeling playful but our partners aren't in a good mood, it's best to respect what they're feeling, because acting too lighthearted may seem insensitive. Also remember that some forms of playfulness are best saved for the privacy of your own home.

Other things you can do to put a smile on your faces. There are so many things you can do to enhance your relationship, but sometimes when you get caught up in the whirlwind of daily living, it's easy to forget what they are. Here are some other things you can do together to put a smile on both your faces.

- Watch "Stand by Me—Playing for Change—Song Around the World" on YouTube. It truly is an experience that will put smiles on your faces. Then find some other fun or amusing things to watch and smile over together.

- Frame your favorite pictures of yourselves. Some may think this is self-indulgent, but being able to see yourself at your best with the one you love will boost your confidence. This is called healthy narcissism.

- Cook a wonderful meal together. It can be for the two of you, or you can invite friends who would enjoy experiencing your vision of the perfect dinner. Get in touch with your inner Julia Child and savor your creation.

- Back in the day, when gas was a buck a gallon, we used to take drives. Jump in your ride, for old time's sake, and take a tour of your neighborhood. Go up streets you have never been on before. Seeing new things around you can take your mind off of your stress.

- Go to your local animal shelter or a pet store on adoption day, and pet the animals. I'm not suggesting that you take one home. The point is for you to give and receive a little love from a homeless animal that needs love. You may decide to adopt, but even if you don't, both of you will be giving some love to another creature, which will make your relationship stronger.

- Get dressed up to go to the store or to run errands. Most people feel better when they know they look their best. Alternatively get dressed up for a night on the town. When you look your best, you'll feel good about each other and the person you see in the mirror every day.

- Read a book from cover to cover, together. You get to relax, be involved in someone else's story, and have that feeling of accomplishment—all while you're being entertained. Fiction is best, but if you're a self-help junkie, that's fine too. Reading to each other can be wonderfully romantic.

Life has so much to offer. As Auntie Mame said, "Life is a banquet, and most poor suckers are starving to death." Finding the playfulness in your relationship may not be possible all the time, but if you put together enough of these enriching moments, you will have a very rich life.

8 *Meeting Needs*

Do you find it difficult to ask for what you need in your relationship? Do you fear it will become a confrontation or end badly? Are you ever unsure about exactly what it is that you need from the person you share your life with? Are you clear with each other about what you each need? Your relationship will prosper when both of you are getting your needs met.

Please understand that there is a big difference between what you need and what you may want. In simple terms, it is like the difference between hunger and appetite. One is a need (hunger), and the other is a want (appetite). You must not confuse the two when you are asking for something from your partner. Make sure that your needs are real, and the one you love will be inspired to meet them.

Your significant other may well respond more often to your needs than to your wants. When you truly need something, the person who cares for you will feel it, and that will inspire her to take action. When our loved ones are in need, we do our best to rise to the occasion. But beware that if you want something "just because," your partner will be less than inspired.

Your wants are something that you have to resolve within yourself; they're not necessarily something your partner has to fulfill. If something is a relationship breaker for you, then please take a look at your motivation. Anyone can get so caught up in their desires that they actually believe they need whatever the object or action is, so be a little careful when you are asking your mate to meet your needs, and make sure they are real.

Perhaps the most difficult part of this process may be identifying your needs. Separating your needs from your wants can be challenging because they may feel the same to you. This is a mental as well as an emotional process. You need to discern your real needs so as not to frustrate your partner or overwhelm your relationship. If you are confusing wants with needs, and thus constantly thinking that your needs are not being met, you will never achieve happiness or balance with your partner.

Only when you are in touch with what it is that you truly need can you bring up the topic with complete integrity. It's also important to make sure that your request is reasonable. Again, if your partner feels that what you are asking for is unnecessary or frivolous, she will not be very willing to make changes for you. You can't ask for the moon, but if you need more romantic time together, you can ask your honey to spend more time with you gazing at the stars. In a deep and loving relationship, your partner will be happy to oblige.

Once you have decided on what you need from your partner, you need to express what it is. If you expect someone to read your mind, you most likely won't get what you need. You'll find that it's easier to get your needs met if you are clear about what you need and show some consideration for your partner.

- Express your needs nicely. You cannot blame your partner for not satisfying your needs if she does not know what they are or does not know that you feel they've been neglected.

- Be proactive and direct. You may need to ask for a hug or for your hand to be held when you are feeling a bit shaky. Getting comfortable with stating and sharing your needs is the first step toward getting them met.

- Get comfortable with asking. To get comfortable with asking for something that you need, remember that it is unlikely your partner will flat-out reject your request. This is about honestly and reasonably stating what your needs are so that you will have a greater chance of having them answered.

- Be as simple and succinct as you can be. Going into a long explanation about your childhood issues probably won't help you in this case. The trick is to talk about your own feelings and to avoid making your partner feel bad because of how you are feeling. Be respectful, and you will find that your needs will get met sooner rather than later.

- Be in the same room. Being in close proximity to another person is really the best way to relay and get your needs met. A phone call can work, but face-to-face contact is really the best way to go. This is about communicating with someone who will listen to what's going on in your heart. Talking about your pain will help to diminish it, and as your mate listens deeply to you, your bond will grow stronger.

- Illustrate what you need with examples. It will help if you are prepared with examples of how much happier you would be if your needs were met, so that your other half will have a better understanding of what it is you need from her and why.

You may feel a little shy about bringing up the subject, and that is actually a good sign because it means that you are being thoughtful about how your mate will receive what you are presenting to her. It usually doesn't work well to drop something serious on a partner without some notice. If your loved one often does not respond well to being asked for things, try bringing up the topic in a softened and nonconfrontational way. Simply asking if this is a good time to talk can work wonders. Alternatively, you can say that you have something you'd like to address as a couple if she has a moment. If she says no, then ask her to name a time that would be better to have this chat. Make sure that you get a commitment to get the discussion going in a timely manner so that you don't begin to feel ignored.

Those who are unable to ask, or who expect others to know, what they need are more likely to become less stable in relationships, as their hearts will remain unhealed. Rather than asking for what they need, they back away or even become irritable, because they don't feel good about themselves.

It would be great if we could all be totally self-contained and not need the emotional support of others. But if life were supposed to be that way, we wouldn't feel the need to receive and give love. When you have good emotional support, it is easier to deal with everything else. When you can't (or won't) feel that support, the weight of your burdens becomes heavier, and your ability to take in the good decreases.

If your partner is unavailable or unwilling to help you get your needs met, it could be a sign that there is some unhealed hurt. Even though you are feeling needy at the moment, you may have to uncover what your partner needs first and then resolve that issue before you can get your own needs met. Sometimes we have to put our own pain on hold while we deal with other issues that require our immediate attention. Though not unfair, this can be troublesome, but usually a little conversation will cure what's ailing, and then both of you will end up getting what you need.

Getting your needs met is not an impossible task. In fact, it is a lot easier than you might think. It all starts with knowing what you need and having a sincere conversation, where you share your feelings in a kind and gentle way. When somebody loves you, he or she will go to great lengths to help you find what it is that you need at the moment. Just ask.

9 Acceptance

Would being able to accept things the way they are make your life any easier? How about when situations or people in your life change? Do you go with the flow, or do you fight to keep things the way they were?

There are two different kinds of acceptance, and both are important in romantic relationships (they also will serve you well in other areas of your life). The first kind of acceptance is taking things for what they are, or appreciating situations at face value. This, for instance, could mean accepting that your partner tends to run fifteen minutes late. By accepting this fact as a fundamental aspect of who your partner is, you'll find yourself feeling less frustrated when he's late.

Accepting your partner for who he is can make all the difference when it comes to resolving issues and solving problems. Perhaps your mate is the type who needs to think for a little while before making a decision. By accepting this fact, you will avoid endless hours of frustration while waiting for him to make up his mind. This may mean learning to understand that you simply need to give him a little space to process his thoughts and feelings.

Accepting the way things are in your relationship is not the same as giving up your desires to make things better. Depending on the reasons why, and how change might look, perhaps the most positive way to deal with difficult issues is to develop the habit of acceptance. Acceptance is one of the tools that will help in almost any situation.

Accepting your relationship for what it currently is and accepting what life hands you can be challenging. But when you allow for differences, individual opinions, and tastes, you will find that they can make conversations more entertaining, broaden your horizons, and make you think new thoughts. It's our differences that make us interesting.

The other type of acceptance is the kind that catalyzes change. It has been said that acceptance is the answer to all of our problems. Through acceptance, we have a starting place to make changes and an understanding of who we (as well as our partners) are and where we truly want and need to be. Sometimes making a list of what is going on for you and how you would like it to be different can be very helpful. It can be even more helpful if your partner does the same exercise. And it is very simple.

exercise: Catalyzing Change

Step 1. Make a list of the things that you feel are not working for you in your relationship.

Step 2. Come up with a solution or two for each of these issues.

Step 3. Exchange lists with your partner so that each of you can understand certain behaviors or circumstances that may be difficult for the other.

Step 4. Deal with only one issue at a time, even if you have several. Avoid taking on too much, so that neither of you become overwhelmed. Once you have decided on what you are willing to change, and you are ready to take action, your relationship will immediately begin to heal. By together catalyzing change, you are clearing the air and making room to strengthen your connection.

Even if you are currently in an undesirable situation, accepting it is the first step toward changing it. Until you are ready to admit that you need to make some changes, you won't. When you see or experience something in your relationship that doesn't work for you, accept the fact that you need to make some adjustments.

Be patient. For example, if you and your partner sit down and agree that you are not making as much money as you'd like, you may need to accept this circumstance as something that won't change overnight. You can then work as a team to identify some areas where you can cut back on your spending, which will help your finances. This approach can apply to a variety of similar situations.

Remember that acceptance is very different from giving up. If your partner feels that you are letting things go, he will try to do the same, or perhaps he will withdraw. Neither of these outcomes is desirable. Discuss what's best for everyone involved, and put some energy into your next steps as a couple.

When couples accept themselves and their relationship not only as a place of comfort but also as a platform for growth, it makes moving forward much more doable. It allows your love to grow, as you accept each other's changes with the passing of time.

Acceptance may be the key to a happy relationship. If you give in on the little things, the big ones usually go your way. Being stubborn will make your life more difficult, and if you are waiting for your partner to make the first move, you both could grow old in the process. Accept that the one you love has a different way of doing things and support him in his efforts. Give a little, and you'll get a lot.

You also need to accept that good relationships are hard work. This means accepting that not every day or interaction is going to be a good one. You have to accept that neither you nor your partner will be perfect, and you need to give each other some room to be human.

Things and people get off track, but usually, with a little time, we all seem to find our ways back. Communicating about where you are and brainstorming ways to make things better are two of your most powerful tools. Of course, you both have to be completely honest about what is going on and what you are willing to accept for yourself and your relationship. If you are patient and communicate clearly, you can make your relationship everything you want it to be.

If someone you care for accidentally steps on your toes, there's no need to get your knickers in a twist. Better to take it in stride by remembering all the times you've made a mistake. No two people can live together and not bump heads upon occasion; this is something that you have to accept as part of life and your relationship. Once you do, you will find it so much easier to deal with the ups and downs of being a couple.

Agreeing to disagree is another form of acceptance. Don't waste your precious time stewing over misunderstandings. It's not about giving in; it's really about moving forward. And remember, making up is much more fun than being upset. Learn to talk it out and lift each other up instead of putting each other down.

Life gets weird, and it's healthier to learn to deal with change rather than denying its existence or turning something into a mini-drama. When you look at your life as a whole, it usually balances out. We all need to learn how to accept each other and our life circumstances, so that we can move forward in a way that enhances our lives and relationships. Make an honest assessment of where you are in your life right now, and accept it. It's the only way you can move to the next level.

Acceptance is an important yet easily neglected habit in relationships. You may want to remind yourself and others in your home by prominently posting a list of some of the best ways to practice it.

Ten Ways to Practice Acceptance

A - Allow for differences.

C - Compromise is key.

C - Controlling behavior is contagious, so avoid it.

E - Enjoy the process.

P - Patience is platinum.

T - Temper your temper.

A - Agree to disagree.

N - Negotiate with kindness.

C - Compassion is key.

E - Embrace the irony.

10 Positivity

Have you ever wondered why some days are better than others or how you can go from a perfectly fine mood to a bad one in a matter of seconds? Do you marvel at couples who seem to let issues roll off their backs? Many successful relationships rely on both parties having a positive outlook on life and each other.

Perhaps the key to keeping harmony within yourself and in your relationship is making the choice to maintain a positive attitude. In many cases, positivity is a choice that couples make, knowing that they have the ability to control their behaviors and even their moods when necessary.

Most people think that you cannot create positivity—that it's either there or not there. This is a mistake. You can definitely encourage yourself and your loved one to be and feel more positive. You just have to learn how to do it. Think about the professional athlete who has lost a game and then has to pump himself and his teammates up for the next one. Coaches can help a lot, so don't disregard professionals, but this is something you can also do as a couple.

A positive outlook begins with believing in yourself and your relationship. It helps to recognize that you are both good people who are deserving of love and kindness. If this is something you have any doubts about, you need to get on the same page as your partner and reaffirm your connection. If you believe in each other and want a positive lifestyle, you must make the commitment to do your best to maintain a positive demeanor in all aspects of your relationship.

This may be easier said than done, but the truth is that you can create a positive relationship as long as both of you want one. All it takes is a willingness to make a few positive adjustments in your attitudes toward life and each other.

As a first step, you need to reaffirm your relationship, which requires communication. You need to make the time to sit down together, have an hour of uninterrupted time, and make reconnecting the only thing on your agenda.

exercise: Reaffirming Your Relationship

Step 1. Sit down together in a comfortable place and look into each other's eyes.

Step 2. Tell your partner that you want to make things more positive in both your lives.

Step 3. Allow your partner to state that she wants to make the relationship more positive as well.

Step 4. Taking turns, gently state one action that you could do to make your lives more positive.

Step 5. Write down your positive steps and post them on the bathroom mirror, so that you can see them every day.

Be specific. Statements like "Just change your attitude" don't work, because they don't give enough direction. Your other half may need you to be more descriptive about what you would like to see from her. Don't forget that this is a "feeling" thing, and it will take more than a moment for you to see and feel the results. Positivity is an ongoing process.

Another great way to build a positive attitude is to center yourself whenever you're not feeling good about your life or your relationship. Once you learn to recognize that you've unexpectedly slipped into a less-than-positive thought process, you can do something (almost anything) to change it.

Here are some things you can do to change negative thoughts to positive ones:

- Take a walk.

- Read a light book.

- Watch something fun on the tube.

- Go online.

- Write down your feelings.

- Play with the dog or cat.

If you are in the middle of a conversation and start to feel negative, take a break from the interaction. Let your partner know that you need a few minutes to adjust your attitude. The trick is not to let the dark thoughts take hold of you. Manually switching your mind and actions to something beneficial or fun will decrease the unwanted thoughts and ultimately make them go away. Then you can replace them with positive actions and thinking.

Another tool for reinforcing positive energy in your relationship is to become more aware of and learn to drop your resentments. Again, it's easier said than done, but I have helped countless couples recognize that they were being resentful toward each other. Changing this dynamic by understanding that your old habits are not working is the key to changing this behavior. It actually will become second nature, once you are aware that you can relate differently and better.

Take the example of Fred and Wilma, whose decade-long marriage was becoming more and more tense. In fact, by the time they decided to try therapy, it had gotten to the point where they were living like roommates.

Wilma had always made more money than Fred did, and though neither of them thought so, they both had resentments about it. Once it came out that Fred felt he wasn't good enough because he brought home less income, Wilma was able to talk about Fred's spending habits and hobbies that she felt she was paying for.

Through talking and some tears, they finally understood why they were behaving so poorly toward each other. Interestingly enough, the conversation inspired Fred to find a higher-paying position, which created a greater balance for them financially and emotionally.

Whether resentment or some other issue is getting in the way, fixing the disconnect makes room for more positivity in your relationship. When there is greater closeness and less conflict, you can't help but feel better about each other.

Here are some ideas for how to create more positive energy in your love life.

- Make a meal together. When two hearts and four hands are preparing a meal, it is food for the soul, not just the body. Make it a fun thing, not a chore, and get into finding your inner top chef. Couples who cook and dine together have more fulfilling relationships than those who fend for themselves at mealtime.

- Take a class together. If you both have the desire and time for growth, you can take a class together and see where that leads you. I know one couple that decided to get their real estate licenses together, even though only one of them really wanted to become a realtor. They were able to support each other through the studying and the test (which they both passed), and then they built a new business for themselves. It didn't happen overnight, but the process made them happier and brought them closer together.

- Volunteer as a couple. Doing volunteer work as a couple can create a great deal of positive feelings in your relationship. Coming together as a couple to help those less fortunate will instill emotions that will only enhance your connection. As you see your efforts make a difference in the lives of others, it will make a difference in your own world and relationship.

- Visualize yourselves as a happy and successful couple. Seeing things getting better in your mind's eye will help bring those changes about. Try this: hold each other's hands as each of you imagines the life that you want. Be reasonable and visualize what you know you can attain and enjoy. Then share your vision with each other. Now together, pick your top five things and describe them aloud as a couple. (Visualization is great when you can do it together, and quite powerful, but you also can use visualization at any time on your own.)

Committing to make changes is a big deal. Making those changes in a positive way, with a positive outcome, is even bigger. Give yourselves the gift of a happy relationship by supporting each other in creating this habit of positivity. Allow yourself to feel good about the person with whom you have chosen to spend your life.

Getting into the habit of being positive and allowing that feeling to flow through your relationship is a wonderful way of going through life with the one you love.

11   Connection

Have you ever felt disconnected from your partner? Do you sometimes wonder where "it" went? Feeling emotionally disconnected from your mate can make you feel very vulnerable and insecure.

Many couples use sex as their main form of connecting. The power of that physical connection can certainly make you feel loved. But there is more to life than what happens in the bedroom, and you need to find other ways to keep your connection going long after lovemaking has occurred.

Couples who do not connect on a regular basis argue more, have less fulfilling interactions, and deal with more relationship issues. The feeling of insecurity that accompanies a poor connection can undermine your relationship by causing you to behave in ways that are designed to combat the insecurity, and you may find yourselves continually in defensive postures with each other.

The sense of a disconnect will make it easier to fight, and the fighting will be less respectful, which can become a relationship hazard. It also will make you less responsive to each other's needs, which will lead to greater resentment.

Connection isn't about sex or taking long walks on the beach. It is about knowing that you have your partner's undivided attention when you are speaking to each other. It's about feeling each other's moods and being able to help the one you love move from a negative to a positive place, just by reminding him that you two have a deep-heart connection.

If you've been feeling distant, reconnecting is easier than you might think, but it does require that you take time to build and maintain your connection as a habit. With our busy lives and the world spinning at speeds above infinity, remembering to put some time aside to cherish the one you love can be a bit of a challenge. But it is totally worth it.

There is a wonderful exercise that can help you develop a deeper connection with each other. I have used this successfully with hundreds of couples.

exercise: Getting Connected

Step 1. Sit where you can face each other and touch knees. Hold hands. Breathe together to increase your connection. Now look into each other's eyes and concentrate on what it is that you love about this person. Allow yourself to appreciate all the little things your partner does for you and how your partner makes you feel.

Step 2. Pause for a moment to absorb what you are feeling, and don't be surprised if a few tears come to your eyes or you feel a little anxious. It's all part of the process. You may feel several different emotions at once. This is perfectly normal and will let you know the areas you need to talk about. Give yourselves a moment or two to absorb these thoughts and feelings.

Step 3. Share with each other what you've been thinking about and what you love about each other. Again, this isn't a race, so take your time and allow yourselves to feel the love that is coming to you. Think of this as a verbal love letter (and you can write one too).

This little exercise and these few words can make your relationship whole again. I recommend that couples who've been feeling disconnected do this exercise every day for a few weeks to confirm their connection and deepen their love for each other. Couples who have a strong connection can handle most of what life throws at them because they know they are facing their problems together, which is deeply affirming. A strong connection with your mate strengthens you and increases your ability to deal with almost anything that comes along.

Feeling more connected will come naturally once connecting with each other becomes a habit. It will become something you look forward to, and something you will miss if it stops.

There are many other things you can do to make and maintain a positive connection with the one you love. These days it is easier than ever to touch base with your partner. Texting, one of the many gifts of technology, is a great way to stay in touch and remind your partner that you are there and that you care, even when you're not in the same place. E-mails work the same way, and perhaps the best long-distance connector now is the cell phone, especially if you can see each other by using a videochat service like Skype or FaceTime.

Sending an unexpected and loving note to your partner will brighten his entire day. With all the stresses of the world, being reminded that you are connected to your partner will decrease your anxiety and improve your day.

Another great connection tool is to surprise your partner in positive ways. Showering him with unexpected gifts of love and attention can go a long way toward making your partner feel more connected to you. Showing that you're involved in your relationship is part of making a good connection, and this is a good way to do it. Of course, it's important to remember special days and dates, but showing up unexpectedly to help or support your mate when he is facing a challenge is a wonderful way to deepen your connection and make it a habit.

Having a great connection does not mean being joined at the hip. It does mean offering to go with your partner to a doctor's appointment if you think he might like your company. Going to the doctor is routine for most people, but if there will be test results and you're feeling anxious, there is nothing better than having a loving partner and an extra set of ears to come along with you.

A big part of a good connection habit is reinforcing that you are there for your partner, no matter what. Don't be afraid to ask the one you love how connected he feels to you, or to tell him how you feel. When you do this on a regular basis, it will strengthen your bond and make you feel more comfortable in your life and your love.

If you have trouble with verbalizing your feelings, please consider that your mate needs to hear the words. And though actions may speak more loudly, it is the soft words that people take to heart. I strongly suggest that you speak your feelings of connection. It doesn't have to happen on a daily basis, but it certainly needs to happen regularly. Affirming your feelings in this manner will solidify your connection so that when troubles occur (and they inevitably will), your partner will feel secure in your connection. Questioning your connection with each other is the last thing you want to have to deal with when you are facing any problem.

Keeping your connection strong is simply a matter of making it a priority. Once you get used to a strong connection, you will want it to grow even stronger. Yes, it's that good.

12  *Honesty*

Do you trust your partner? Do you ever get suspicious or insecure for no good reason? Have you ever questioned your loved one's behaviors but not said anything for fear of hurting her? Is honesty an important value in your relationship?

Trust in your partner can be defined as knowing that your partner's intentions are honorable. A lack of honesty can erode the foundation of a relationship, leaving a couple confused and insecure about their connection and life. It creates a dynamic where either one or both of you may feel uncomfortable asking for help when you need it, because on some level you don't trust your partner to give you the support you need.

Couples without a high degree of honesty suffer from low morale because they have become used to concealing their weaknesses and mistakes. Their time is spent behaving for effect rather than working together toward positive outcomes. If you don't feel that you can tell your partner everything, you have a problem that will only worsen in time, so you'd best get around to fixing it as soon as possible.

When you know you can totally trust your mate, it removes a large potential for worry. It builds your sense of emotional security. You feel better not only about your partner but also about your life. Having an honest relationship creates a kind of buffer between you and the difficulties of the world. When you have a mate you can trust and rely on, it's easier to take those risks that help you grow.

The habit of honesty can be created at any time. Of course, it's best if your parents instilled it in you, but even if you are a little challenged with telling the whole truth, you can learn and be rewarded for making honesty part of your relationship and your life. Here are a few ground rules.

- Telling the whole truth builds trust. One of the most important rules for building and maintaining honesty is to always tell the whole truth. Being open and honest about your thoughts and feelings helps to ensure physical and emotional fidelity.

- You should never have to question your mate's integrity, fidelity, or behaviors in the world or in your relationship. Honesty isn't about sharing your misdeeds after the fact; it's about being truthful and trustworthy in all your actions to begin with, so that you never have to "fess up."

- A culture of honesty means being honest all the time. Many people feel that telling little white lies to spare their partner some grief is okay, and in some cases that's true. But you can't have a culture of honesty only some of the time. If you tend to omit or color the truth, to make things look a little better, it could actually damage your relationship on a deeper level. Trying to protect your partner or trying to avoid looking bad in her eyes can create more trouble than it's worth. It is best to be aboveboard in all your dealings.

- Honesty can be tender. If you have to say something to your loved one that may be unsettling, do it as gently as possible. Brutal honesty has gotten some press lately, but I have seen it do more damage than good. You need to temper your honesty with some degree of kindness. You can be honest without being harsh. Choose to be gentle, or your message will get lost in the hurt feelings that result from the harshness.

Both of you will be much more able to communicate if your hearts are safe in the process.

Honesty is not just about telling the truth. It is about telling the truth in such a way that your partner will hear it and benefit from it. We all want to hear how great we are, but we may need to make some slight adjustments in how we do things. This is where a little honesty from someone you love and trust will help you make changes that can make your world a better place.

To get yourself in the right frame of mind, you can imagine yourself as a coach and imagine that your partner has just shared (or wants to share) a presentation she's written. The following exercise will show you how to give constructive criticism.

exercise: Coaching Your Partner

Step 1. Sit up straight and listen attentively to your partner as she speaks.

Step 2. Stop and think before you respond. Remember that your tone and approach matter if you want to give constructive feedback.

Step 3. Begin with something positive. For example, tell your partner that she did a great job.

Step 4. If you noticed some room for improvement, ask your partner if she wants some constructive criticism before you give any. Never start off by saying "Hey, you left this out!" or "This didn't work."

Step 5. If the answer is yes, then give your feedback in positive terms—for example, "I think if you add such-and-such, it would be even better." Be as specific as possible.

This approach usually works. If you start using it with each other, you will appreciate having someone in your life who can be a wonderful mirror for you and can tell you truly what it is you need to hear.

When asked about what qualities they want in a partner, most people will list honesty high among them. Most of us at some point have had a friend or family member lie to us, or even worse, had a dishonest partner. When you have a relationship and a family, you need to know that everyone is on the same page, and that is hard to do unless both of you are honest about what's going on.

What honesty gives you is a great deal of comfort. Knowing you can implicitly trust your mate allows you to be your very best self. With this foundation, your relationship will continue to thrive, as you are able to give each other the positive energy you need to navigate life's ups and downs. You can feel honesty. It is an extra lift in your world.

Being completely honest with each other means that you can share more. It also means that you have more choices. If your partner wants to do something that you'd rather not, you need to be honest and let her know how you feel. Then put your heads together and come up with a compromise, so that both of you can enjoy the experience. For example, don't tell your partner that you are really looking forward to going bungee jumping if the idea totally terrifies you. Be honest about how you feel. You can go with your partner as support, but you don't have to jump. In fact, by telling the truth, you'll have more fun, because you won't feel resentful that your mate has dragged you into something that made you very uncomfortable.

This scenario actually happened to me. In the end, I did take the leap, though when we had first discussed it, I declined the offer. When I saw the understanding in my partner's eyes, we became closer as a couple. Perhaps that's what gave me the confidence to jump. We came away feeling better about our union and ourselves.

Honesty makes your relationship a win-win. When you're a couple and only one of you wins, it's the same as lose-lose. Both of you need to feel heard and respected and give honest feedback so that the relationship can grow to its full potential.

If being completely honest is something you have difficulty with, you may need to look at the reasons why. If you do not know how to change your behaviors, for your sake and the sake of those you love, get some in-depth counseling to help you understand and correct them. It will improve your relationship and your life.

Honesty is a way of life, not just a behavior. Keeping it paramount in your relationship will bring in more goodness and hold the bad stuff at bay. Knowing you can totally trust each other offers a type of freedom and comfort that really helps your relationship work in the best way possible.

13 Nurturing

Have you ever wondered how people keep their relationships going so well while dealing with daily life? Do you marvel at how some couples seem so close and connected? We all need nurturing, but just as individuals need it from one another, your relationship needs to be nurtured too. Those who are adept at nurturing their relationships have longer and happier relationships than those who do not.

The concept of nurturing a relationship may be a bit confusing at first. Nurturing your relationship and nurturing your partner may seem to be the same thing, but there's an important difference. If you look at your relationship as three entities gathered together—you, your partner, and the relationship—the concept is easier to understand. Each of these entities needs to be nurtured, and it is up to the two partners to nurture their relationship as well as each other.

Being able to nurture the "us" part of your life can be a little complicated with kids, work responsibilities, and life being as challenging as it often is. That is why it's so important to make nurturing a habit. The good news is that nurturing can become almost second nature. It feels so positive when it's working that you want to keep doing it. Your goal should be to make the positive habit of nurturing (both the one you love and the relationship that binds you together) part of your everyday behavior.

Nurturing can be hard to master if you didn't experience enough of it earlier in your life, but once you get the hang of it, it's easy and quite pleasant to do. It all starts with a desire to be closer to the one you love. And if you have that desire, the very first step you need to take is to tell your partner that you want to be closer to him than ever before. You should avoid being pushy, so say this in a manner that conveys how much happier you both will be once you're both nurturing your relationship.

When you express your desire to nurture each other and your relationship, you are confirming the deep feelings that you have for one another. By taking action, you are changing how you feel and relate while giving yourselves the strength and heart you need to make your time together the best it can be. Nurturing builds trust.

Nurturing behaviors are easy to practice, and though some may require a little more effort, the payoff is well worth it. Think of your relationship as an interest-bearing account. Once you put more energy into your relationship, it pays bigger dividends like contentment, excitement, joy, and desire. In fact, you get back much more than you put in. Here are a few nurturing actions you can take.

- Make a date night at least once a week. It doesn't have to be lavish—just some space for the two of you to spend some quality time together. To be happy as a couple, you need to have couple time, so that you can be adults together every so often. Once date night becomes a habit, you will not want to let it go.

- Carry out little acts of affection. Things like holding hands or walking arm-in-arm create the ties that bind. I know people who feel out of balance when their partner isn't physically touching them in some way. Also important are little touches as you pass by each other in the house; never ignore a moment when you could lovingly nurture your relationship and your partner. These little things become very strong parts of a loving relationship.

- Keep in touch throughout the day. Talking, texting, and e-mailing are some of the easier ways to let your partner know you are thinking about him and about being together again. Being physically apart does not mean that you have to be far away from each other emotionally. Learn to carry the love with you during your workday, because it makes life a little sweeter.

- Remember special dates. Remembering special dates and events in your relationship, and sharing those memories and days with the one you love, is a big part of a happy and close relationship. The memories of certain times are kept not only in our heads but also in our bodies, for our cellular memory is very strong. When positive actions remind us of even more positive memories, the experience becomes quite powerful and bonding. As a couple, having and celebrating special days nurtures your relationship. Enjoy them.

- Remember your deepest feelings for each other. Your relationship requires food for the soul to nurture it. You need to get in touch with each other at the deepest level you can reach. Trust that your closeness is what will give you the strength to defend your relationship against the difficulties that you will face together at some point. No relationship is completely trouble-free, but if you regularly nurture yours, you will have a much better chance of avoiding problems that could rattle it to its core.

Knowing that you are loved gives you strength. Your relationship, when in proper working order, also gives you strength. The value here is that you can forge a very powerful partnership when both of you are feeling secure in your relationship. It can give you the ambition you need to tackle almost any issue that comes your way and give you the confidence to take on new challenges, especially if your partner could benefit from your actions. Sometimes we want greatness not for ourselves, but for those we love.

Making sure that your partner knows he is loved is another component of the habit of nurturing. And people receive love in different ways. You need to talk with your partner and find out what messages you are sending and how they are being received. If your mate is not feeling the love you are sending, you need to find the way to his heart (by asking) and then give him the love he needs in the way he can receive it best.

Some people are great at receiving compliments, while others cannot take them in. Many people respond to gifts, others to actions, and still others to warmth. The one you love will be able to give back to you much more easily when the two of you can share what it is that makes each of you feel nurtured. This simple communication has the ability to make your relationship much more close.

Every successful relationship needs the care and nurturing of two committed adults, giving to each other in a way that creates a mutually beneficial connection. Just as we need to breathe to survive, your love needs nurturing to flourish. Giving your relationship what it needs to thrive is a truly loving gesture. Make the effort: you are both worth it.

Ten Tools for Nurturing Your Relationship

1. **Kind, constant, and honest communication.** Your relationship will not survive if you do not talk. The more you communicate, the closer to each other you will be.

2. **The willingness to work through difficulties and disagreements.** Throwing in the towel, even if you don't walk out the door, is not the path to happiness. You must face the discomfort that comes with differing opinions and ideas.

3. **A sense of humor, some fun, and a bit of distraction from the rigors of daily life.** You can't spend all your free time working on your relationship—don't make it a hobby. Discuss what you'd like to do, where you'd like to go, and how both of you like to have fun. Then go do it.

4. **Sharing life lessons.** When you discover something about life, or you make a self-correcting move that is healthy for your relationship, let your partner know. You'll be surprised by the positive response.

5. **Emotional support, validation, and compliments.** Feeling that your partner likes and respects you makes for a strong connection. You have to lift each other up and let each other know the depth of your caring.

6. **Love, intimacy, romance, and sex.** These are the cornerstones of a loving relationship. Being great roommates just won't cut it. There has to be the desire to be together as a couple. If the spark has gone, there are innumerable ways to rekindle it. All you have to do is try.

7. **Sharing goals and dreams that resonate with both of you.** We are happier when we are working toward a goal than when we have achieved one. Make sure you always have something to look forward to and that you are pursuing it as a couple.

8. **Compassion, acceptance, and forgiveness.** These will show you the way through a difficult time. If you are together for a while, there will be losses, challenges, and some things that you just can't fix. Weathering the storms together is a big part of what relationships are all about.

9. **A mutual desire to step outside the box.** The tried-and-true is good, but the never-attempted-before may be better. Couples who share new experiences together develop a stronger bond.

10. **Being able to admit mistakes and talk about them.** We all screw up. Learning to understand and let go of mistakes that you or your partner make will turn your life around and give you more time for joy.

14 Balance

Have you ever wondered why on some days you feel so much love for your partner and on other days the energy is not as strong? Do you have moments or days where you can't feel the positive vibes, your mood is a little down, or you find that your partner is irritating you for some reason?

This is the normal pattern of most relationships. By understanding that there will be these ups and downs, and by learning a little about relationship housekeeping, you can get through those times when you can't feel the love you know is there.

Love is not constant. It waxes and wanes like the moon. Having an argument or feeling bothered by your partner's demands or desires doesn't mean that your relationship needs to go in the recycle bin. It means that you have to understand and talk about the natural course of feelings that ebb and flow throughout emotional connections.

When the feelings are at low tide, remind yourself that this is a normal and natural part of your relationship, so that it doesn't throw you off-balance. Keeping love alive is a lot like keeping a body alive. You have to breathe to live, and sometimes you have to give your relationship a little breathing room and let some issues resolve themselves (most small ones do). If you aren't feeling the love at the moment, tell your partner that you are processing your feelings (with a smile on your face and in your heart), and don't send out any bad vibes. Remember, your feelings come from *you.* Your partner, though involved, cannot process your feelings for you. But you can talk them out together, which usually ends up making both of you feel the love and be better for it.

Some people have trouble knowing whether what they are feeling is love or not. Loving someone is very different from the heady feeling of being "in love," which is, frankly, just temporary insanity. Truly loving is more a sense of knowing that you are with someone who's got your back and won't turn her back on you.

When you are with someone who embodies the qualities and values that you admire, and you think that maybe you could love this person but can't seem to bring yourself to say the words, or really allow yourself to feel it, there could be deeper issues. Fear of rejection, memories of a previous abusive relationship, or even a need for independence can make you want to keep a fire escape open in your heart. The problem is that by having an exit plan, you never really get to experience the potential fulfillment in taking the risk of letting someone in.

Once you do let someone in, your life will never be the same. This person is now imprinted on your psyche forever. We've all had love and lost it, or suffered from a broken heart. It may be why some of us recoil at the thought of deepening a loving relationship.

You've probably been told that it isn't wise to put all your eggs in one basket. But if you try to play Easter Bunny and hide a few for later, you're not going to get the true benefits of what love really is. So let yourself love and be loved. The trick is to be very careful with the basket. Don't hedge your feelings when it comes to love, because you won't get out of it what you want.

Some people hold back because they fear they can't return the love that's being offered or because they fear they won't know how to help love thrive. There is no one answer. You have to keep trying different things, get into deep conversations (and learn to like them), and make a commitment to love your partner unconditionally. I also suggest recommitting on a daily basis in your own head and heart, and sharing those feelings with your partner. Couples who do this have stronger connections.

Holding back is a means of self-protection, and sometimes that's understandable, but if you want a real relationship, you have to share all of your emotions, good and bad. By sharing what is going on for you, you are letting your partner know what she can do to make things better for both of you.

Some couples find that, while it can be deceptively easy to get their relationships back on track after a normal disagreement, it's much harder to keep things moving forward, especially when unexpected events derail them. It's important to remember that even the most stable relationships experience turmoil. Difficulties and distractions are part of life, and they can't help but have an effect on our relationships. Instead of ignoring the issues or arguing, you should confront them head-on and with an eye toward the future.

Many couples make the mistake of equating a good love life with a balanced relationship. Having a balanced relationship takes more than good sex. Maintaining a satisfying relationship requires regular attention and upkeep in all areas. All you need to do is take ten minutes a day to check in with your partner. Just as a successful physical fitness program requires a lifelong commitment, when it comes to emotional fitness, it's impossible to overstate the importance of regular relationship maintenance.

And make sure you don't overlook opportunities for creating greater balance and harmony.

- Cherish your partner. When your mate feels your love and knows that you will be there through thick and thin, you've got a very strong foundation.

- Be a great cheerleader. We all need to know that we are the star players in the eyes of the people we love.

- Let your partner know you love her. Appreciate what you have and show it. Life without love is only tolerable. I really think that being in a loving relationship is the only way to truly experience life to its fullest.

- Remember to check in with your partner regularly. Some couples need this more than others, but it's always good to check in with your partner, whether or not you've experienced something upsetting.

- Spend quality time together. Enjoying your time together is important for all couples but especially important for those who are feeling overworked and disconnected or distant. Making time for each other can help you regain your balance.

- Get good at forgiveness. Taking a moment to forgive the one you love is an important part of finding balance. It doesn't matter what the issue was; giving yourself and your partner the gift of forgiveness will lighten your burden and make your love life a little sweeter.

These little things can make a big difference. Emphasizing the positives in your relationship will help you maintain a good and loving connection. It will give you greater balance as you cope with common challenges, like the state of your finances, raising children, or even an unexpected illness. Once you incorporate relationship-enhancing techniques, like good communication and forgiveness, and begin to change any negative behaviors that cause problems in your relationship, the issues will become more manageable and your connection will grow deeper.

While talking through problems doesn't always take away the pain, communicating gently and effectively can help you avoid certain pitfalls and keep unnecessary issues from coming up. Most successful couples have certain behaviors, skills, and practices in common, and the most essential of all is communication. This is the most important thing in your relationship. If you don't take the risk to speak what's in your heart, it will become too heavy. Your true feelings will leak out, and that usually happens in inappropriate ways.

When couples are experiencing relationship difficulties, the journey toward healing can be so emotionally complex that they may lose the ability to identify their feelings. If you hurt each other, talk about it and make the appropriate apologies and changes so that you don't do it again. Apologizing appropriately can be one of the most healing things you can do to reconnect. What most couples don't know is that conflict is normal, and learning how to deal with it can be a milestone on the path to a healthy relationship.

Learning and practicing these love lessons will help you each be the best partner you can be. It's worth the effort. The rewards are a full heart and a full life. I know it's scary to love like you're not going to get hurt, but it's the only way to get the goodies from the most wonderful of emotions.

15 Togetherness

When you're far away from your partner, do you sometimes feel uncentered? Have you longed for more quality time with the one you love, yet you can never seem to make it happen? Do you find that you function better when your mate is nearby?

Making togetherness a habit will help you feel better all the time, even when you can't be together. From my perspective, there is nothing finer than the sense of togetherness as you journey through life with each other. Now that is a habit worth creating.

Togetherness is not the same as codependency. It's not the same as having someone around to help you combat your insecurity or to make you feel more comfortable in your own skin. Togetherness is the act of two people creating a life together yet still being independent when they need to be. Togetherness means that your other half completes you and that when you are with him (or even when you are apart), you experience this wonderful gift of wholeness through your relation-ship with him.

We all want to be with people who keep us level-headed and unafraid. We also want to be with people who make us feel we are our best selves and who can bring out our most loving and caring qualities. When two people can do this for each other, and be together in this way, it opens up many doors. Togetherness makes you emotionally stronger so that you have the fortitude you need to tackle life head-on.

When you are working and raising a family, it may seem that you are doing all you can to keep your love life together. But there are so many things you can do to increase your closeness and get more out of your relationship.

Yes, it can be a challenge when your boss piles a bunch of extra work on you or when the kids are sick, and you are being pulled in twenty different directions at once. Togetherness is a bond that gives you the extra strength you need to accomplish what you need to do and still have some energy left over to enjoy life and cherish the ones you love.

Togetherness begins with the commitment to use your time together in a positive way. Save issue resolu-tion for another time, and, yes, you can schedule time to be with each other. If you haven't done this before, all you have to do is ask your partner to name a good time to meet up to chat. And don't make the asking seem too heavy. Tell him that everything is fine and that you just would like to have this time together. If you both enjoy it, you can schedule this communication time regularly into your day or week. Solid couples communicate regularly.

Another great togetherness tool is to set aside times of the day when you connect with each other (see chapter 11). These could involve sending a text during your coffee break, calling at lunch, or e-mailing in the afternoon. When we know we're going to hear from the one we love, we have something definite to look forward to, and that makes getting through even the most challenging day much more rewarding.

Couples who are strong in their togetherness seldom need to question their partner's fidelity, honesty, or integrity. There is an understanding that you are with each other for a higher purpose and that you belong together. This sense of belonging can be so powerful that it lifts your life and your heart to the next level.

Here are some other useful ideas for developing the habit of togetherness.

- Show up at a business event as the loving spouse. This is all about giving. Staying in a supportive role and praising your mate's efforts to everyone you talk to will make your partner feel uplifted and loved.

- Snuggle up close with the one you love. This works whether you're watching TV together or reading aloud from the same book (it also works if you're reading two different books). Sitting across the room from each other in separate chairs may feel comfortable to your body, but it does nothing special for your heart.

- Cuddle at bedtime. Cuddling helps sustain a long-term loving connection. If you need your own space for sleeping, that's fine. Just hold each other for fifteen minutes before you go to your side of the bed—and, by the way, those who engage in this activity have healthier sex lives.

- Share the little things. When you share the little things, in addition to the big ones that you can't help but work on together, it creates positive feelings that help to maintain your love from day to day. It also makes it easier to lean on your mate when things get a little tough.

- Make plans to be together. Making plans to do something special or fun together will make you feel closer to each other if your partner isn't available at the moment. It also will give you something to look forward to.

If you think that your relationship could benefit from more togetherness (and most relationships could), you need to state your feelings. If your partner looks at you inquisitively, tell him that the closeness you have is wonderful, but that you'd like a little more. Then describe what areas you feel you could excel in if you had more of his energy around you.

Be sure to explain that this isn't about being in lockstep. It's about growing the emotions you have for each other and reaping the benefits. All that you have put into your relationship will be enhanced when you foster your togetherness.

Remember that this is a proactive step. It's not about sitting and waiting for your partner to do something that makes you closer to each other. It's about making the things you think and talk about a reality. Don't just make plans for the occasional vacation. Make regular plans and schedule them in on your calendar. When special occasions come around, make sure the two of you have a few minutes to be alone together, so that you can have a moment or two of your own. This kind of time together sustains the happiest couples.

Another great togetherness tool is to check in with yourself when you become upset because your partner is not available. You partner isn't breaking the together-ness habit. Life is simply getting in the way, so be under-standing. You will be able to share everything with him when you have the opportunity to be with each other once again. And it is perfectly fine to tell your partner that you missed him but you were okay because you knew that you would be reconnected soon.

If you are regularly engaged in this habit, you will have a much easier time getting through those moments when you really need your other half but he can't be there. This habit prevents resentments from building, because you have the understanding that you are together, no matter what. Even if you can't be with each other during a time of need, the strength you have gotten from your relationship will help you get through your difficulties until you can face them with your partner.

I know many couples who could be described as inseparable. It's one way to be in a relationship. But you don't have to be in physical proximity all the time to garner the benefits of togetherness. The feeling will stay with you through good times and bad, when you're together and when you're on your own. It is a sense of belonging and being involved, which will make you feel better about yourself and your relationship.

You are not giving up your independence here. Rather, you are aligning your soul with the soul of the person you cherish and love. You are not giving up who you are, what you do, or any of your dreams and desires. You are making a choice to love and be loved by your mate, and if you allow it to bring you as close together as possible, you will discover that you have found what you always wanted.

16 Problem Solving

Are there issues and problems in your relationship that you are unable to deal with? When problems arise, do you argue or do you go to your separate corners and pout? Ideally, when a problem comes up, do you commit to solving it together?

Don't be afraid to deal with problems. In fact, you should be more fearful of problems that are left unsolved. Every couple has troubles, and the only shame is in not facing them as they arise. If you let issues fester, your whole relationship can become infected. Deal with your troubles now, and you'll save yourself a ton of grief down the line. If you get bogged down and can't seem to move past your issues, professional counseling is in order. Don't avoid issues or live with something for months that could be more easily handled with the help of a trained and objective third party.

Often the problem with problems is that they don't come along one at a time. They generally appear in clusters. When one is taken care of, another pops up to take its place, and you wonder to yourself, *What did I do to deserve this?*

No, it isn't karma—you aren't being punished—it's just life. Considering economic woes that we can't seem to fix, issues that arise in any normal relationship, and the unexpected upsets that besiege our days, it's understandable that there will be times when our moods, or those of our partners, will reach low points.

No quick fix or Pollyanna affirmation is going to change things. The truth is that you have to trudge forward until you can change things for the better. Perhaps someone else can help, but chances are they can't take away your troubles. This is where creating the habit of problem solving can make a big difference in your relationship.

While no magic bullet is going to suddenly make everything better, the input of a loving partner can help. It feels good when the person who touches your heart can help you navigate your issues. In fact, if you don't seek help from your mate while you are struggling with personal or professional problems, it can be a burden on your relationship. You have to learn how to talk about your problems. Remember, the one who loves you is on your side, and even if the issue is one over which you disagree, you are still a team.

Give your pain a voice, and let your partner listen. You will be amazed at how much weight will be lifted from your shoulders. Here are a few tips for how to share what's going on.

- Get over your pride. Not wanting to look bad in the eyes of the person you admire may keep you from sharing what's on your mind. The truth is that if someone loves you, she will help you deal with your dilemmas. Talking about it can help shed light on how to get through a problem. That's how therapy works too.

- Get some perspective. There will always be problems, but sometimes we don't have the capacity to handle them all by ourselves. Getting a 360-degree view is impossible when all you can see is what's going wrong. Talking with your mate can give you some much-needed perspective.

- Brainstorm with your partner. You may find new ideas to help you move forward. Besides getting new ideas, when you brainstorm with your partner, you're receiving the emotional support you need to face what's in front of you, rather than having to face it all by yourself.

- Lighten your load. If you have been sitting on your stuff to the point where it's starting to hurt, it's time to let it out. How to do it is up to you, but keeping your pain inside will eventually lead to some kind of meltdown. Sharing your problem with your mate will ease the load for you.

- Write it down. It can be helpful to dictate what's bothering you to your mate while she takes notes. Seeing the issues in writing, as well as getting your mate's feedback, will give you greater clarity, which can help you see your way through your dilemma much more easily. You can then prioritize what's most important to work on first, then second, then third, and so on. As you do, you can create a checklist to use in resolving issues, which will help you take action.

Learning that it's okay to talk about relationship problems can feel a bit like a trip to the dentist for a toothache. You know that the discomfort will stop once you get the tooth fixed, but you don't want to go through the process to begin with, because it hurts. And sometimes, with emotional issues, you may be embarrassed to share what's really going on. But you need to get over it, because it's so important to talk with your mate. It's the only way to get the comforting and nonjudgmental emotional support that will help you solve these issues.

Having someone to help you solve your problems reduces the anxiety that comes with most situations that are out of your control. Knowing that your mate will be there to console you and offer her support gives you more energy to face things head-on and approach a reasonable resolution. This exercise will help both of you arrive at answers more effectively, as you make problem solving a regular habit.

exercise: Solving Problems Together

Step 1. Admit and define the problem. Exactly what is it, really? Now ask yourself if you are a part of the problem and also ask yourself if you are blaming your partner. By understanding your thought process, you may find that a simple attitude adjustment could make things much easier.

Step 2. Ask clarifying questions until you completely understand the problem and each other. Ask as many questions as necessary to cover all the bases, so that you have the answers you need to move forward.

Step 3. Create solutions. First ask yourself what you may not be seeing or what isn't clear. Greater clarity will help you see ways out of the dilemma. Now start making a list of possible solutions.

Step 4. Evaluate your ideas. Make a list of necessary resources and weed through your ideas. What is the probability of success for each of your choices? Pick the three best, and then pick the one you would like to try first.

Step 5. Create an action plan. Decide where and when you want to make your first move, and take an inventory of what you can do to help you solve the problem. Then execute your plan.

You will be amazed by the progress you make once you approach your problems as part of a team with your partner rather than alone. I cannot tell you how much easier it is to confront issues when you know you aren't facing them by yourself. Do not try to shelter your mate from your problems, but learn to share that part of yourself, so that you can deal with whatever is going on together. Having a loving partner to talk to when the chips are down is one of life's greatest gifts.

Note that if you are working through a relationship problem and have hit a wall, it's wise to take a break and cool down. Take about twenty minutes to an hour before you return to the problem together. If you can't seem to get a resolution, come back to it tomorrow when both of you have had a chance to sleep on it and allowed the triggering issues to settle. Taking a break will help both of you think more clearly and will keep the problem from escalating into an argument.

Problem solving with the one you love is very effective, but it also can be very emotional, especially if it has to do with your relationship. Learning that by working together, you can tackle almost anything will give your relationship a stronger platform from which you can both grow. Knowing that you can solve problems together will make both of you feel safer and closer.

Remember, too, that not every problem has to be solved. Some problems resolve themselves and others just go away. Having some patience helps, and reminders of that can come from the one you love. All you have to do is listen.

17 *Affection*

Do you ever wonder about the quality of your connection or about what's going on when the two of you have long gaps of not demonstrating your affection for each other? Most people want and need affection, but what do you do when it isn't flowing freely in your relationship?

The affection that you exchange with a loving partner can turn bad days into good ones and make your troubles seem much smaller. Without it, your ability to take on the world can be greatly compromised.

Many of us desire more affection from our partners, yet we fail to communicate and demonstrate this desire. If you have had a long period of being off-course, rebuilding affection may be a bit of a challenge. At first, neither of you may be feeling it. But take heart, because saying to each other that you want and need more may be all that's required to get things going in the right direction. When we're distant from those we love, they feel it. The road back can be awkward, but all the two of you may need to move forward is a brief discussion and a long hug.

Often in our busy daily lives, we fail to see opportunities to embrace our love. I believe we should all do our best to find, act upon, and treasure the moments when we can exchange affection with the people we love. You can think of it as being on a scavenger hunt where you're looking for every opportunity to hold each other and feel the loving energy that your partner has for you. Once doing this becomes a part of your regular life, you will get so used to it that when your partner isn't around, you will feel the distance and long for his presence.

The most important affectionate moments are those that happen outside of the bedroom, like reaching your arms around your partner's waist and giving him a squeeze when he is doing some work around the house or holding hands while you walk. There are countless ways to exchange affection, and much of it isn't even physical. Here are a few ideas for how to demonstrate your affection daily.

- Give a dozen hugs a day. In America, we do not touch each other as often as we need to. There are surprisingly few couples that give each other a dozen hugs a day. Ask yourself how often you show your partner affection, and see if you don't need to increase your daily dose. Couples who have a good balance of affection have fewer instances of anger and fewer arguments.

- Remember to express your affection verbally. Giving words of encouragement and endearment, leaving little notes, and sending loving texts are a few examples of how to show your partner affection. We all need to hear as well as feel that the one we love loves us back. Expressing your feelings and thoughts of love to your partner can bring a smile to your heart; it also can defuse difficult moments.

- Brag about your partner to others. Everyone likes to hear the person they love talk about them in a positive light. Listening to your partner tell someone else how wonderful you are is going to make you feel good about yourself and about your relationship, and when you brag about your partner to others, it makes him feel the same way. Verbally praising your love in front of other people is a big part of showing affection.

- Remember to say "I love you." We all need to hear that we are loved. Yes, it is true that actions speak louder than words. But if there are no words at all, we can get a little lost. Affectionate words are like an emotional compass guiding us back home to our hearts.

- Perform random acts of kindness. Doing little things for your partner is a great way of building your affection bank account (and you never want to overdraw this one). Being affectionate to your partner can be as simple as opening a door or bringing home something you know he has been wanting. Cooking a favorite meal or taking him out to a favorite restaurant is another way of showing affection to the one you love.

What happens in the bedroom is also very important. Engaging in romantic behaviors and good sex helps most couples maintain a healthy balance in other areas of their lives. If the romantic fires have been burning low lately, there are many ways to get them going again. It starts with a desire to be romantic and some communication. From there you can take it just about anywhere you want. Approach this area playfully and remember to listen to your partner as you explore each other and find new ways of relating. Couples who gently explore each other romantically have a connection that can withstand the test of time.

Ten Tips for Keeping the Romance Alive

1. **Be aware of your partner's needs.** Most people with great romantic lives are more concerned with pleasing their partners than themselves. When you are a giving lover, the pleasure will come back to you many times over.

2. **Acknowledge small acts of romance.** It is usually the little things that make a big difference, like little kisses, pulling out chairs, and taking each other's arm as you stroll to the movie theater. Letting your mate know you like these actions will keep them coming.

3. **When you get a romantic idea, share it.** Perhaps you want to do something totally unusual, or maybe there is an adventure you have always wanted to participate in with your mate. Doing new things helps increase your bond and your romantic intimacy.

4. **Don't be afraid to deal with shyness.** Every couple has those moments. As we age, our bodies change and we notice different things about ourselves. We can become shy about asking our partners for affection when we've been a bit adrift. Don't be afraid to ask. Your partner will probably be grateful you did.

5. **Think of one thing that would make your romantic life better.** Whether it's trying something new or something tried-and-true, share with your partner what you'd like to do. Ask your partner to do the same. Compare notes and then go for it. You will both be smiling afterward.

6. **Be demonstrative and show that you care.** All the words in the world cannot convey what is communicated in a deep and passionate kiss. Caresses, holding hands, and other forms of light affection actually deepen a relationship and should always be a part of your connection.

7. **Appreciate the gesture, even if the timing is a little off.** If you rebuff your mate, it may be a while before he tries again. If you aren't in the mood at the moment, give your loved one a little kiss and say you will be ready later. That way your lover has something to look forward to.

8. **Be sure to talk about sex and what's comfortable.** Those couples who do not communicate about sex have less satisfying romantic lives. Appropriate boundaries make you feel safe, and you can always change your mind.

9. **Give it time.** If it's been a while since the two of you have exchanged affection, you may need to spend a few nights just cuddling and feeling close to each other. For many, that is as intimate as sex. For many couples, cuddling leads to sex.

10. **Feel the bond with the one you love.** Trust the love that you feel and the person who is giving it to you. Feeling the deep connection that you have with your lover will make kisses deeper, lovemaking more passionate, and life better in general. Being connected with the one you love in this way is one of the most powerful and pleasurable experiences you can have.

If you'd like more affection in your relationship, you need to communicate and demonstrate to your mate what you would most enjoy. If you are the one doing all the giving, fear not. With a little talking, you can easily change this dynamic and together build the mutual habit of affection.

Let your partner know the types of affection that work best for you, and ask what he needs. In this way, you will discover new ways of being affectionate with each other. Once both of you have committed to making this an everyday habit, you will find different and pleasant ways to connect and shower each other with the kind of affection that will make your friends green with envy.

18 *Compassion*

Have you ever wanted more compassion in your relationship? Is being compassionate a part of your value system?

Compassionate people are happier people. Compassion, which is a combination of empathy, concern, kindness, and consideration, is central to a fulfilled love life. Couples who are compassionate with each other have more joy and understanding in their relationships.

When you are sad, a compassionate gesture from your mate, such as a warm hug or words of encouragement, can make all the difference in your mood. When someone takes your hand and gives you the emotional support of just being there for you, it can ease your pain, no matter what it's about.

Without compassion, a relationship can become hardened, and when that happens, your interactions will be less caring, and you may start to build up resentment and feel like you're in the relationship all by yourself.

Developing the habit of compassion is not difficult. All it requires is a mutual desire. You will want to talk with your partner to explain what your needs are and to ask what her needs are in this area. Being compassionate toward each other becomes much easier when you know exactly what to focus your energy on.

The next part is a little more challenging, because you need to make the commitment to always talk together in a compassionate manner. There is no room for harshness in a compassionate relationship. If any negative behavior surfaces, you will need to identify it and shut it down, so that you can get back to relating in an appropriate way.

You can consciously practice compassion every day until it becomes a habit. The good feelings you get from it will make you want to have more. The depth you feel in your relationship, when you know how much your mate cares, is palpable. And the habit of compassion will change how you relate; you will become softer and more considerate toward each other—and that is a plus for any couple. Here are some ways to get started.

- Demonstrate your concern. Being compassionate is good, but expressing your compassion is even better. When your mate is sharing an issue with you, you should show that you're there for her and that you really care about what she's going through. You partner will feel it and be able to return this concern in kind.

- Look into each other's eyes. This action has been highly romanticized—it's in the movies— but it's seldom carried out in modern relationships. We are usually looking at the television instead of each other (even when we're making love). Looking deeply into the eyes of the one you love and feeling her emotions is going to create more depth and compassion.

- Be a good listener. An important thing to remember is that we all hold sad memories, and when your partner has feelings about something that happened long ago, why not offer compassion? Ask her about those feelings and the circumstances surrounding them. Being a good listener, and hearing and responding to what's being shared emotionally is one of the most compassionate things you can do for another person, especially someone you love.

- Be nice to each other. Another way to create the habit of compassion is to focus on being nice to each other. Remember how, at the start of your relationship, you both took those little extra steps to be considerate? They still work, and taking these steps again will improve your intimacy as well as your dynamic. Everyone values a little kindness, and doing nice things for no good reason will make your bond stronger. Plain and simple.

- Be extravagant if you want to. You can do big and wonderful things that your partner doesn't expect, but in the long run, it's always the little things that make the difference. No one can be expected to be over the top all the time.

- Be there for your partner. When your partner is down in the dumps, maybe there's a particular reason for her sadness, or maybe the one you love is just having a bad day. Whichever is the case, when you are soft and nonjudgmental, your partner will take in your love, which will help to temper her mood. One of the best parts of being in a relationship is having someone show you some empathy when things aren't going so great. Consider yourself lucky to have this gift in your life.

Another way to build compassion in your relationship is to show compassion for others. Doing volunteer work as a couple can make your relationship stronger. I know many partners who feed the homeless, do Meals on Wheels, and find various other ways to help those less fortunate. The experience makes them feel closer to each other. Some bring their entire families. My partner and I do this kind of volunteer work; it makes us feel like we are contributing to the well-being of humanity, and we respect each other more for putting out the energy. Doing community service as a couple can be fun, and it is something you will never regret. By showing compassion to others, you are showing your mate the part of your heart that makes her love you even more. Being with a compassionate mate makes you feel proud of your relationship, which in turn makes your bond stronger.

The Dalai Lama said, "If you want others to be happy, practice compassion. If *you* want to be happy, practice compassion." To help you remember how to practice it, you can prominently post a list of ten characteristics of compassion somewhere in the house where you'll see it often.

Ten Characteristics of Compassion

C—Caring. Being there for your mate in a time of need is really the essence of your humanity. If someone you love is facing challenges, when you show your compassion, you lighten her burden as well as strengthen the bond between the two of you.

O—Oneness. Adhering to the philosophy that we are all connected can make what you're dealing with a bit easier. Feeling as thoug you are one with the person you love can ease the burdens of life.

M—Miracles. I have seen too many miracles to believe they don't exist. Miracles happen every day. They reaffirm our spirit, leave us amazed, and give us a reason to keep going. Just be open to the idea.

P—Patience. Sometimes getting what we need takes more time than we think it will, but it helps to know that we are moving in the right direction. Little affirmations along the way can remind your loved one that she is getting a bit better every day.

A—**Acceptance.** Sometimes we may not be completely ready for what we have to handle in life or are called upon to give. Accepting that the right things are happening for the right reasons, at the right time, with the right person, makes difficult transitions easier to manage.

S—**Strength.** Giving and receiving compassion makes us stronger. As a giver, you need to maintain your personal strength, so that you can continue to provide what your loved one needs.

S—**Support.** When we can't find our own strength, the support of those who love us may be what we need to get through the day. Just having your partner there for you, even if you're only watching TV together, is life affirming.

I—**Imagination.** Knowing exactly how to be compassionate can be a challenge. This is where a little creativity can be very helpful. You don't have to be a doctor or a nurse to care for someone in pain. When you put your minds together, you have even more power to create what you want and need.

O—**Openness.** Being open to emotions allows us to feel things we might ordinarily block out. Through compassion, we are able to sense depths we have never experienced before. Growth can take place at every moment of life—and it often comes from the people we love.

N—**Nurturing.** Perhaps the essence of compassion lies in our ability to be nurturing. Most of us probably don't get enough nurturing. Being able to help your partner feel cared for is an incredible gift.

When you show compassion, you express your feelings in ways that you might not necessarily be able to express in words. Those who give compassion freely have the most fulfilling relationships. Developing and exercising the habit of compassion creates a safe zone for your love and for all the feelings and issues that may arise in your life. You cannot replace the soft touch of your partner and her sympathy with anything else. It will heal both of you and give you more emotional security than you could ever imagine.

19 *Thoughtfulness*

What does thoughtfulness mean to you? Is it about your partner giving you things, or is it about what he does for you from his heart? Would you like to increase the level of thoughtfulness in your relationship?

If so, there are many tools and techniques that you can employ. Thoughtfulness is a habit that can make the difference between having good interactions with your mate and being in a relationship that's falling apart. I have worked with numerous couples who could be in great relationships, but they have forgotten to be thoughtful of each other, and the resentment has built to the point where therapy is no longer a choice but a necessity.

I know about the demands of working forty-plus hours a week, raising kids, keeping up with the bills, and maintaining a home. By the time evening rolls around, you hardly have any energy for each other, and weekends are not much better. When you're overworked and overtired, it's easy to start thinking that you're doing everything all by yourself. The truth is that your mate is probably working just as hard as you are and may be feeling similarly.

Yes, it's easy to forget that you are in this together, but if you remind each other to be more thoughtful, you will be better for it. Have a little talk with your partner about how you can be more thoughtful toward each other. Your conversation need not be heated or sad. All that's needed is a mutual desire for a more thoughtful relationship.

Once you've expressed this mutual desire, any number of actions will make it work. Creating the habit of thoughtfulness will improve your relationship, and having the initial conversation is often all couples need to get themselves back on a positive track. Here's an exercise to get you going.

exercise: Conversing About Thoughtfulness

Step 1. Starting the conversation about making thoughtfulness a habit can be a bit daunting, but remember that you are not making big demands here. You want to talk with your partner about various ways you can make each other happier. With that thought in mind, approach the subject softly, so as to minimize any defensiveness on your partner's part. Be sure not to make your partner feel guilty or unappreciated when you make your request.

Step 2. Share with your partner the things that he's done in the past that made you feel he was thinking of you. Once he realizes that he has been doing most of what you need all along, it won't seem overwhelming or laborious to him. Thank him for doing all of these things for you.

Step 3. Gently suggest any new areas where you may want him to make some extra effort.

Step 4. Ask your partner to give you some examples of what you've done for him that he's especially liked in the past. Then ask him to tell you other ways in which you could be more thoughtful toward him.

Step 5. Allow each other to take in what's been said, and then make a commitment to be more thoughtful of each other.

What's great about this exercise is that it will help both of you feel more appreciated rather than less. It will inspire you to take what you've learned and use that information to be even more thoughtful toward each other. This process works, so give it a try.

Thoughtfulness can be expressed in lots of ways. Focusing on being a little kinder to each other is the most important and can make all the difference in your relationship. One couple I know has developed a ritual where he always opens the car door for her, and whenever he does, she gives him a little kiss.

Remember when you were first dating and you used to do little things for each other all the time? How did it make you feel? Isn't that part of the reason you are with your current partner? All I'm suggesting is that you continue doing these things long after you have both checked into your retirement villa. If you've forgotten how, here are some ideas to get you started again.

- Make the first move. To get the ball rolling, why not be the bigger person and make the first thoughtful move? It can be as simple as a compliment. Compliments have a way of lifting people out of the doldrums and into a place where they are much more available to participate in their relationships, and most people never seem to hear enough of them.

- Make life easier for your partner. Some people hate paying the bills; others can't stand making vacation plans. We each have our own peccadillos, but having the presence of mind to take a burden off your partner's shoulders—now that's thoughtfulness. Your partner will respond appropriately by doing something similar for you.

- Do nice things for no reason. Doing nice things is such a healer, and it creates a lot more love in your life. If you do something nice for the one you love, he is likely to return the favor. I'm not talking about buying Super Bowl tickets or diamond bracelets. It's all about the little things, like leaving love notes, lending a helping hand, or asking your partner to dance in the living room when nobody's watching.

- Do for your partner as you would have your partner do unto you. Think about how you want to be treated by your partner, and do those very same things for him. You may have to tweak it a bit. Your mate may not be into having a manicure/pedicure, though he may love the idea (and feeling) of a foot massage.

- Listen more closely. If you listen closely, the one you love will usually reveal what would make him feel really good. Oftentimes our partners tell us what they desire, but for whatever reason, we don't hear them or we forget too easily. When you hear him express what he wants, make a mental note of it, and when you get the opportunity, grant him the favor.

Sometimes thoughtfulness doesn't require anything more than acknowledging when something is important to the one you love. Perhaps he had a bad day at the office. Offering some compassion and letting him know that you are aware of how hard he works, and that you appreciate everything he does for you and your family, can help lift him out of a potentially uncomfortable emotional spiral. In the same respect, thoughtfulness means truly hearing what your partner says to you. If he opens up to you about something that's hurting him or causing him stress, be sure to really listen. Your partner always wants to know that you care about his life and what's going on in it.

True thoughtfulness comes from deep within your heart. When you really love someone, you want him to know it, and thoughtful actions (no matter how tiny) are a great way to show that you care. Your mate will feel it in a way that will deepen the intimacy in your relationship.

One of the best parts of this loving habit is that, when it becomes integrated with your heart and soul, you will feel as good as (if not better than) the person who's on the receiving end of your thoughtfulness. The beauty of it is that it gets stronger every time you use it. Getting through any rough patches also becomes easier when you know that your mate is there for you, no matter what.

I live to give, and I think about things I can do for my loved ones on a daily basis. I do get a kick out of putting a smile on someone's face—especially if that someone is the love of my life.

No matter what's going on in your world, you can take that extra step and think deeply about how you can brighten your partner's life. Both of you will be better for it.

20 *Respectful Arguing*

Do arguments with your partner sometimes become uncomfortably loud and unnecessarily hurtful? Have you ever discussed the value of fighting fairly and where the two of you may go wrong?

When discord is ever-present in a relationship, there is little room for enjoying life together. The resentment can be so thick that everyone else notices. Friends may even try to avoid you, because they don't want to get caught up in the emotional destruction derby. Many people see negative behaviors and bad vibes as something to steer away from, and you may be feeling exactly the same way. If so, you need to take action.

To begin the healing process, both of you must get out of denial mode and admit that a problem exists. You will have to put your differences aside so that you can begin to really talk about what's been going on. Breaking out of this negative pattern will require a new game plan. Maybe it's time to see a counselor. Perhaps apologies need to be made.

If things tend to go badly when the two of you have a disagreement, know that many couples struggle with this. But also know that conflict in relationships is perfectly normal, and the key to resolving disagreements is to learn how to fight fairly. This means learning what needs to be said, how to say it, and what not to say. Learning to state your needs without adding fuel to the fire is a necessity. Respectful arguing is a skill as well as a habit. You can learn how to use certain communication tools that will help you build the habit of respectful arguing. All it takes is practice.

- Before talking with your partner, make a brief list of all the things you want to say. That way, even if the conversation doesn't go in the direction you are expecting, or gets a bit off track, you'll be able to address everything that you need to get off of your chest.

- Focus some of your energy on always being polite. This focus will help you avoid reacting to things that might trigger a defensive response. Always avoid making verbal attacks, using bad language, or criticizing your partner in any way. Being polite will help to maintain your partner's and your own self-esteem and ability to focus on the real issues. Use kind and understanding language to indicate to your partner that you are coming from a well-intentioned place.

• Focus on getting clarity. Getting clarity can be difficult when emotional issues arise, but it's important. Sometimes our feelings take over, and we get scared by them, or blinded by anger. Being open and honest with your partner, even if you are anxious or hurt, is the best way to resolve your issues. Say what you need to say so that you can move on and enjoy your life, or even just your day, together.

• State what you need to say through I-messages. Express how you feel, such as, "When you say (or do) this, I feel this way." Using I-messages will help your partner be able to listen without getting defensive. If there are behaviors that you need your partner to change, use solid examples along with gentle suggestions of how you would like things to be different.

• When it's your turn to listen, don't interrupt. The key to having a great conversation is to be sure that each of you listens when the other speaks. You can agree ahead of time that neither of you will speak while the other is talking.

- After either of you speaks, ask the other person to restate what was heard. After you speak, give your partner the opportunity to restate what she heard you say. If she heard you correctly, then hearing her say it will be reassuring and healing. If she misheard you, then go ahead and clarify what you wanted her to hear. (Again, don't interrupt but allow her to finish speaking before you make the correction.) Likewise, after your partner has given her side of the story, restate what you heard her say. Then give her the opportunity to tell you if what you heard is correct.

- Take a time-out, if necessary. Taking a time-out is a tried-and-true method of keeping things on track. Either person can call a time-out, but you need to agree beforehand that you will commit to completing the conversation, no matter how uncomfortable it may become. Leaving things unfinished is an invitation to further misunderstanding and hurt feelings.

These tools really do work. Familiarizing yourself with them and using them whenever a disagreement comes up will make a huge difference in how you communicate, whether or not you are having a disagreement. Finally, it always helps to remind each other of your commitment to the relationship. Promise each other that you are going to work through whatever difficulties you have, and that you will use warmth and kindness as you work on making things better. As you make this promise, make sure you are hearing and feeling everything that your partner is saying.

Developing the habit of respectful arguing may not be as simple as it sounds. In fact, you can count on this project requiring some consistent effort. The reward will be a relationship that's consistently on a positive track and moving forward.

21 Security

If you have been through a bad relationship, where there was dishonesty, anger, or perhaps even infidelity, you may be more inclined to worry about the relationship you are now in. If you feel any distance from your partner, even if it's a passing phase, you may begin to feel insecure in your relationship.

If you are someone who has been through a difficult issue like cheating, certain behaviors—like your mate coming home from work later than usual or spending more time on the computer—could make you worry. You could easily think, and perhaps start to feel, that the person you love and trust is being unfaithful. More than likely what's going on is that the economy is forcing your partner to work harder than usual, or perhaps the two of you are just a little bit disconnected from each other.

The best way through this is to have a conversation and, without accusing your partner, to gently ask for clarity. Asking for reassurance is not a sign of weakness. Being able to admit that you are feeling a little insecure at the moment is a good thing. A loving partner will not be offended (though a little defensiveness is quite natural). If you ask for compassion, the one who loves you should be able to give you the reassurance you need.

If the person you care for is having a difficult moment, being there for him is really what true love is all about. Think about all those times when you have reached out to a loved one. Have you ever been turned down? Has there always been a hug when you needed it?

As you look for explanations for feelings of insecurity, you also should ask yourself if you've been acting a little distant too. If so, it may explain why you're feeling out of sync with your partner.

Insecurity in a relationship comes not only from the present but also from the past. Talking about what's bothering you will lead to greater trust, which will bring about a deeper connection with your partner and help to lessen your pain. Once our lives become intertwined with others' lives, they become more complicated, but we have a new source of stability and understanding. I can't think of a better reason to be in a relationship. Love will wax and wane, but your commitment and your willingness to be there for your partner is what makes life work in complicated times like the present.

Once you get the conversation going, it will probably flow much more easily than you anticipated. If your mate is feeling a little off too, he will welcome the opportunity to eliminate the discomfort for both of you. Many times, our loved ones are not aware of what we are feeling. If we don't share feelings of insecurity with each other, it will lead to greater insecurity and disconnection. So take this step of giving yourself and your loved one the chance to make it all better, and start the conversation.

You may discover that you can't have your partner around as much as you'd like, either because his work responsibilities have increased or because he has other commitments. If this is making you feel insecure, you can create greater balance in your relationship if you develop some other sources of support.

- Rally your emotional support structure. If your partner is less available than you'd prefer, there's no reason to spend your time alone. Spend more time with your friends and relatives. Being reminded that you are loved by your family and friends can be good for your relationship, because it will make you feel more secure in yourself. Both you and your partner will appreciate this change.

- Seek professional advice. If you are having a tough time emotionally, you may want to seek counseling. If your concerns are financial, a financial adviser can help steer you in the direction that you want to be heading. There are good people out there, and if you don't have someone, ask a trusted friend for a referral.

- Join a support group. If you are comfortable with support groups, there are a ton of them out there for any issue that you might have. Do a local search using your favorite online search engine, and you will find dozens. Sometimes the positive energy of a good support group is just what the doctor ordered.

- Appreciate the good things in your world. Too often when we are down, we focus on worst-case scenarios. Instead, think about all the people and things in your life that make you happy to be alive.

Many people bump along in their relationships until they feel some sense of insecurity, and then they live with it or they act out because of it. It's much better to develop some habits that foster emotional security. If you do these things a few dozen times, they will begin to come naturally.

First off, keep your feedback short and sweet. If your partner does something that makes you feel insecure, like forgetting to say good-bye in the morning before he leaves for the day, it is your responsibility to your relationship's good health to let him know. I would recommend that you send a text simply saying "Missed kissing you good-bye today," and leave it at that. You will get a reply. He may or may not mention the forgotten kiss, but, regardless, know that you have planted a seed and then give it a moment to grow. Sometimes we have to teach our partners (and ourselves) what it is that we need to be the best mates we can be.

Another behavior that leads to the habit of security is to look inward before confronting your partner. If your mate has always been positive and has never given you a reason to doubt him, then take that in. If you are feeling insecure, it's good to take a look inside yourself first for what might have triggered that feeling. It may be that you were disturbed by a movie you watched the night before, and you unconsciously may have projected difficult feelings on to your partner when he forgot to call at the usual time. When you watch a disturbing film late at night, it can easily slip into parts of your brain that can cause you to feel insecure. And this is just one example of how outside influences can alter our perceptions of the ones we love.

Knowing your partner deeply and trusting that he hasn't changed will remove any reasons you may have to doubt his actions. Unless he gives you a direct reason to mistrust him, you should always try to give your mate the benefit of the doubt.

Finally, a little reassurance never hurts relationships. Saying "I love you" should be returned in kind or with special words that the two of you have chosen to mean the same thing. Good communication is the most important thing in a relationship. So let your partner know if you are running late and how your day is going, and ask for this favor to be returned. This is more than just common courtesy. It is an act of kindness that keeps the one you love from stressing (perhaps about things he shouldn't).

 22 Enjoyment

Do you feel that you are getting the most joy that you can out of your relationship? Are there things you have thought of doing to increase your level of enjoyment? Do you feel that you have to push your partner along in order to experience the joy in life?

Joy can be elusive, especially when your relationship has hit a few speed bumps along the way. But finding joy can make the difference between success and failure, not only in relationships but also in life. Joy is a feeling that comes over you when you look at your partner and feel all the good that the two of you have created together. This is how life should be.

Sometimes we get so busy with our daily lives and responsibilities that we forget to enjoy our journey together. Other times, what we think we want may overshadow the simple enjoyment of living together and appreciating what we have. Many people have discovered that they don't need a big house and new cars to have a good life. Couples have become closer to each other than ever these days, as the world has become more difficult to navigate; and they need the emotional support of a loving and devoted partner. With this closeness comes the added benefit of more love to draw upon, which can only serve to strengthen you and make your life together easier. The result is greater joy. And the more joy you feel, the stronger your relationship is, which will bring you even more joy, and so the cycle goes.

There is no one right way to experience or bring more joy and positive energy into your love life. Whether it's doing new things together or relishing the tried-and-true ones, there are numerous ways to make enjoying yourselves a regular habit. You may want to begin with something small, but remember, the world is your canvas. Once you allow yourself to experience more joy, your mate will see it in you, and it will change the way you relate to her. When you're happier, the one you love will be more cheerful around you. You also will find yourself more open to trying new things. As you do enjoyable activities more often, even those unpleasant chores that you have to do will become easier, for you'll have something to look forward to after finishing them. Here are a few ideas for how to bring more joy into your relationship.

- Talk, e-mail, and text daily. I can't emphasize enough the importance of keeping in close contact throughout the day. It will make the two of you feel closer to each other—and it does wonders for your love life. And I'm not talking about sending a text reminding your partner to pick up the dry cleaning. Your messages should be reminders to your partner that she's on your mind when you're not with her. It's always a source of joy to know that your partner has been thinking of you.

- Say "I love you" at appropriate times. Again, hearing the words makes a difference to most people. You may think that your partner already knows, but the truth is that everyone wants verbal reassurance. As a couple, you can come up with your own special language to express this sentiment.

- Make plans to do something you love with the person you love. You may not be able to do something every day, but knowing that you will soon have an opportunity will give both of you something to look forward to, which makes for more joy in the relationship.

- Learn to let go of old grievances. If you are holding on to anger toward yourself or someone you love, learn to let go of it. As simple as it sounds, we all know that letting go of anger takes self-discipline, patience, and plenty of internal strength. The benefit is that as you release the rancor, you will rediscover and open your heart to more warmth, affection, and joy.

- Spend more time together. Whether your relationship is new and you need to give yourselves some time to get to know each other, or you've been together forever, it's important to spend enjoyable time together as a couple. It doesn't really matter what you do as long as you're enjoying yourselves. Whether you're quietly hanging out and reading together or you're disclosing a piece of your history (or something that happened just the other day), spending this kind of time together will bring you closer together, guaranteed.

- Never underestimate the power of kindness. Some people believe that being kind is a weakness—nothing could be further from the truth. Kindness can make the difference between success and failure. It can make your life and relationships deeper and more meaningful. It also can change the lives of others in a very profound and positive way. Kindness is a very powerful tool. Simply responding to your partner in a pleasant tone, even if your team didn't win the big game, is a tool that will serve you better than any you ever bought in the hardware aisle.

- Order a meal from your favorite restaurant. Give each other a break, and instead of cooking dinner, order takeout. While you're at it, break with the rest of your nightly routine. Instead of worrying about bills or the next day's work, free up some time to rent a movie that you've been meaning to see together. An occasional departure from the norm will make your relationship feel refreshed.

- Take on a project together at home. You don't need to remodel the entire kitchen. Pick up some paint and change the color of a room that needs a facelift. You could be brave and attempt to build (or assemble) a new piece of furniture together. You'll bond over the challenge, and you'll get to share the excitement of completing the project. Plus, the result—a little change of scenery in the home—can be a source of pleasure, especially when you did it together.

- Go through your photo album. Spending some time together looking through old photos will bring back happy memories. It not only will remind you of all the joyful times you've shared with your partner but also will encourage you to do more things together that you enjoy.

- Appreciate your partner's company. If you are going out to a movie, be sure to appreciate this opportunity to spend time with your partner. The same thing goes when your partner surprises you with a gift of some kind. Take it in and really treasure the gift as well as the energy that was put into this surprise. Yes, it is the thought that really matters.

Perhaps appreciation is what people in relationships enjoy most. To make appreciating each other more of a regular habit, take the time to stop thinking about everything else, and focus on your partner and the life you have built together. Soaking up the joy is something most of us can get better at. And when you learn to increase your joy, your relationship will get better and better.

Given all the hard work it takes to make a good relationship work, you deserve some joy. It is here for you as long as you don't harbor resentments, and you share your real feelings. The things that prevent us from feeling joy are the same things that create depression. We have to get out of ourselves and into the hearts and minds of the people we love. Only then can we share the truly joyful gift that life as a couple can be.

Making enjoyment a habit may be one of the most fulfilling things you will ever do as a couple. As you embark on this path, know that the joy you feel will radiate out to others, and you will have deeper relationships with all of the important people in your life.

23 Emotional Progress

Have you ever felt that your relationship has gotten stuck? Have you ever thought about what it would be like to take it to the next level? Have you invested the time and energy it takes to move your love life forward?

No couple gets along all the time. Trust me, you will bump heads more than once, but don't let this hinder your emotional progress as a couple. Stagnant relationships can often leave one or both partners feeling bored and disconnected. The trick is to continue to grow as a couple, fixing relationship issues along the way as a healthy means of strengthening your bond.

Emotional progress is a practice employed by the most successful couples. All it takes is a commitment to keep growing. Once you make that commitment, you will find different ways to stick to it.

Visualization is a great way to move your relationship forward. If both of you spend a little time every day thinking about what you want your relationship to be like, and what you'd like to get out of it, you can actually move it in the right direction. Thoughts inspire actions. Visualizing what you want can help you create new magic in your relationship, even if you were thinking that the magic might be gone. Visualization can make a big difference in your lives, and it's even more powerful if you do it together.

exercise: Visualizing Progress

Step 1. Sit down with your partner in a comfortable place, facing each other and holding hands. You can close your eyes.

Step 2. Create a picture in your mind of what you want and need. Your partner should do the same. Spend several minutes with these images, or allow other images to come to mind.

Step 3. Share your vision with your partner, and ask him to share his with you. Discuss how your two different visions can come together as one vision.

Step 4. Take several minutes to visualize your future together.

Visualizing progress will help you create positive results by literally imprinting what you desire on your brain, thus increasing your motivation to make the positive changes you want. Visualization also relaxes you and encourages you and the one you love to be closer. Doing this together and sharing your dreams will make it that much more effective and powerful.

Bringing up the topic of emotional progress may be hard if you think your partner may not see things the way you do. Even if your significant other feels similarly, it can be a little challenging to broach the subject of "emotional progress." Defining it can be hard, but you know it when you feel it. Probably the best way is to gently suggest to your partner that the two of you will be happier if both of you help your relationship continue to grow.

Once you're on the same page with your partner, you can use the visualization exercise from this chapter. Alternatively, the two of you might prefer to evaluate where you are in your relationship and contrast it with where you'd like to be. By doing this, you'll be able to identify what you could add to your relationship to achieve your goals. Writing down your goals can help too. If both of you find that you'd like some growth in specific areas, developing the habit of emotional progress will be much easier than you might think.

It's also always a good idea to do a little emotional housekeeping to keep your relationship in good working order. Doing this will help you to continue to grow emotionally and not get stuck in a rut.

- Never take your relationship for granted. If you think you may have been making this mistake, take the brave step of asking your partner if he feels taken for granted in any way, shape, or form. Appreciation of each other is essential. You both may revel in doing your own things, but always be a team when it comes to your union.

- Always show consideration and respect. We all know when we are in a bad mood, but why do we have to inflict it on those we love? If you need to hide under the covers for a day, go ahead, but at least be nice about it and let your mate know what's going on.

- Be aware of your circumstances. If money has gotten tight and you have had to put some of your dreams on hold, talk about it. Both of you may be feeling some frustration, but discussing where you are in life can give you the perspective and security you need to move forward.

- Go easy on your partner, even if you're not always getting what you want. Asking nicely is always a good idea. But if you try to control your relation-ship, you aren't going to have much energy for anything else. Sometimes you will have an easier time moving forward with your partner if you can let go of something that's bothering you.

- Don't sweat the small stuff. Be careful that every issue doesn't become as dramatic as the last scene in *Titanic*; drama just plain wears you out. If you are making mountains out of molehills, something is missing from the relationship. Find out what it is and start giving it to each other. Your relationship should be a place of peace, not a stage for controlling the attention in the room.

- Take responsibility for your own happiness. No matter how hard your partner tries, he or she cannot create happiness for you. This is an inside job, pure and simple. If you want to blame someone for making you unhappy, look in the mirror.

- Let go of past torments. Letting go of old com-plaints may be the greatest gift you can give to your relationship and to yourself. Just think of how much lighter life would be without all the excess baggage you carry from being inadvertently offended.

- Never lie about or fake happiness. Faking it will impede your progress. Be open about your failings as well as your successes, and always tell the truth if you feel bad about something that has happened or that you've done, so that whatever it is can be forgiven and dropped. Only when both of you are open with your thoughts and feelings can you truly achieve emotional progress as a couple.

- Trust that you are in this relationship for growth, and never stop looking for it. Couples who gently explore each other simply get more from life together.

Making emotional progress is not only good for the health of your relationship. It is also good for your physical health. People who continue to grow in various areas of their lives live longer and stronger. Those who withdraw usually end up lonely and wishing they had done more to change their circumstances.

Happy couples know that doing things differently, and with a commitment to being the best they can be, is a huge step in keeping everyone and everything on the right path. From here, you have nowhere to go but up.

24 *Working on Your Relationship*

Are there things in your relationship that simply don't work for you? Have you ever wondered why some relationships work so well and others don't? Have you looked for ways to make your relationship work better?

There's a reason why some relationships do so well. It's that the couples in these relationships actively work on them. Some do therapy, others read books and discuss them, and still more have frequent talks about the state of their relationship so that there is no guessing or concern about each other's actions.

I once saw a cartoon featuring a curmudgeonly-looking couple, both wearing scowls. The caption read, "This relationship works because we make it work!" I know it was meant to be a joke, but the truth is that if more couples did a little work, divorce attorneys would work a lot less.

Working on your relationship is not effortless, but it is a lot easier than repairing one that has gone wrong. This idea of working on a relationship is foreign to many couples. Many people think that problems will straighten themselves out if they ignore them. So after an argument, for example, couples won't discuss the problem or work to resolve it and minimize the fallout. They simply go on with their lives until they forget about what happened or something else comes along to distract them from the issue. The trouble with this is that ignoring problems tends to cause a buildup of negative feelings. When the right trigger comes along, those feelings resurface, possibly causing a much bigger problem than if the original one had been handled properly.

Another very important thing to keep in mind is that your partner is not a psychic—if she does something that you dislike and you bottle up your feelings rather than say anything, then don't expect her to know what you're thinking. It would be unfair of you to blow up at her if she did the same thing again. But, of course, blowing up is never a good idea. A much healthier course of action is to gently let your partner know whenever she does something that upsets you.

Another tool I have used for years is the weekly relationship meeting, which is adapted here from my first book, *Emotional Fitness for Couples*. If you have no experience with this kind of meeting, you should know that it is a gentle process and takes much less effort than having a fight. It's a powerful tool.

exercise: Conducting a Weekly Relationship Meeting

Step 1. To begin with, ask your partner if she would be interested in having one of these meetings, first, to see what it would be like for the two of you, and second, to see if you can get anything out of this time that will help your relationship. Most people want their relationships to improve, so asking this question—in a nonthreatening way—usually works.

Step 2. Agree to follow some important ground rules. First of all, keep it polite. That means no raised voices, no belittling, and no bringing up past grievances. If you want to bring up something that bothered you in the past, save it for another meeting where you plan to discuss old issues. Your weekly relationship meeting should concentrate on events of the last week. Again, these weekly meetings are designed to help you relate to each other in a positive manner, so it's important to behave appropriately.

Step 3. Begin your conversation by telling your mate that you are grateful that she is doing this with you, and let her express her feelings about starting the process as well. If it feels right, you can do the connection exercise from chapter 11.

Step 4. If you have any issues, tell your partner how you are currently feeling. If something has been bothering you about how you've been relating, this would be a good time to talk about it. Be sure to state your feelings through I-messages. Once you have finished, allow your partner to share her own feelings or issues. Warning: Please don't try to get everything on the table at once. Tackle only one or two issues at a time, or easle what could be a productive interaction will become overwhelming.

Step 5. After both of you have had the opportunity to speak, express to your partner what you heard her say, and listen to what she heard you say. Misunderstandings often can be cleared up with a little feedback and communication.

Step 6. Drop any negativity you are holding on to, and hold each other instead.

Conducting a relationship meeting on a weekly basis will keep most problems from festering. They will be over before either of you has a chance to build resentments. Nipping it in the bud, as they say, will lower your chances of things going wrong and feelings getting hurt.

You also need to be able to work on older issues and to talk about how to make up for those times when you have inadvertently hurt your partner. Sometimes we are not aware of what's been going on until something else triggers a feeling, and we get painfully reminded of some old hurt. Old issues need to be discussed and resolved in a different format from the weekly meeting.

One of the best ways to clear the air is to write down what is bothering you and what you would like your partner to do to make up for it. As part of this exercise, you should also write down things that you've done, if you suspect that your actions may have caused your mate some pain. Read what you have written and refine it so that you can present it to your mate in the kindest way possible. When we are asked nicely to make changes in our behavior, it is much easier to adjust our attitudes and actions.

Working on your relationship can be fun as well. For example, another great tool for working on your relationship is to make plans for your future together. If making long-term plans seems like too much to deal with at the moment, then you can make plans for your next vacation or for next year. Look at all that you want for each other and discuss the reasons why. You will learn intimate details about your mate and her desires, and you will have a chance to share what you would like from your partner to help you feel more fulfilled.

Making plans allows you to take a journey together that opens up emotional doors. When you can see the hopes, dreams, and desires of the one you love, and then help bring them to fruition, you're creating a very positive dynamic, and the two of you will feel the progress you are making as a couple. Making plans also gives you something to look forward to together, which is very bonding.

Working on your relationship can mean working on a joint project, such as creating your own business together. You can make a little extra money while spending more time with each other. From having weekend garage sales to starting a garage band, working alongside the one you love is a wonderful experience, and often it enhances your connection because you are doing something together as a team.

Building positive routines as a couple is another way to work on your relationship. The more you do together, the closer you become. If you both like to exercise, find a way to do it together as often as possible, and have dinner together as often as you can. Having dinner together as a couple—and with your kids, if you have kids—is a time to come together to share your days and your dreams. If having dinner together is not a habit, I strongly suggest that you make it one. I cannot overstate how important this seemingly little thing can be.

Working on your relationship doesn't have to be hard—and it can be fun—but it does have to be done regularly for the two of you to get the most out of your time together. Couples who choose not to work on their relationships usually aren't very happy in them. Make the choice to do what's required to cement your bond, and make your life together as good as it can be.

25 In Love for Life

Has it always been your fantasy to meet the man or woman of your dreams and to live blissfully together until death do you part? The problem is that about half of all marriages end in divorce. Breaking up is, at best, a painful process, and most of us have had more experience with it than we care to remember.

It has been known for a very long time that those in healthy marriages or long-term relationships have lower mortality rates and better immune systems. Now scientists' new research shows that those fortunate enough to be in loving, committed relationships experience lower stress levels. So who wouldn't want love when what you receive from it is soul-warming affection and a longer life?

Even after a very difficult time, couples who work at it can put the love back into their relationships. To some couples, this comes as easily as realizing that they have become distant from their partners. For other couples, the work is a little harder. Remember that making this happen takes the desire and effort of both partners. This chapter will review two of the most important tools for building your bond with your partner. It will then introduce a new tool to try. Here are the three tools.

- Having good and frequent communication. Communicating well and often with your partner is perhaps more important than doing anything else in your relationship. Communication lasts longer than any other thing between the two of you, so you'd best get it right.

- Maintaining positive relationship traditions. Another thing that will keep you in love for life is keeping up positive relationship traditions like a fancy date night or a casual weekly movie. So often, happiness comes from having little things like this to look forward to.

- Taking time together at the end of the day. The importance of spending quality time together cannot be overemphasized. One way to do this is to take time together at the end of the day. After the dishes are done, your children are in bed, and you still have a bit of energy left, decompressing with your mate can be a bonding experience.

The last of these tools is worth expanding on. Couples can sometimes become so busy doing their own things apart, or even be so busy together with household tasks and work, that they don't make room for downtime. Busy couples live much of their lives separately, and part of what makes relationships enjoyable is the process of coming together again.

It's nice to take some time while both of you are still awake and not yet in bed. This way, each of you will get a chance to talk and be heard.

You can drink tea together or share a glass of wine before going to sleep. It's a calm and pleasant time to tell each other about the different things you did during the day. however, this is not a good time to bring up relationship issues. Rather, it's an enjoyable time to be with each other and share the positive side of life.

A nice chat while resting in your lover's arms will make your whole relationship more enjoyable. This little bit of regular sharing at the end of the day can keep your connection strong, and you'll sleep much better. Sleeping is also a time of intense closeness, though few think of it this way. I believe that more consciousness may be exchanged with a partner when you are sleeping than when you are romantically engaged.

Sometimes we forget what a powerful force the closeness we get from our relationships is. It can help us slay the dragons of the day or inspire us to build a castle for the ones we love. And it all starts when someone you care for cares back and lets you know it.

Connecting at the end of the day doesn't have to take long. Go with whatever is comfortable, but put your chores, ideas, and work aside to bask in the glory of your great decision: to be with this person who shares your life and bed.

Having that time together will help you deal with the following day. If you do this consistently, you may find your attitude brightening. Relaxing together at the end of the day does help many people release their pent-up anxieties, and it can make dealing with difficult people or situations at other times less stressful.

Most importantly, taking some time together before bed gives you the reassurance and emotional bonding that will help you keep your relationship moving forward.

If you are stuck or feeling at odds with your partner, share this tool with him, and see if you can find some time at the end of each day to be together. Commit to a week of connecting this way before you evaluate its success. This ritual may not be for everyone, but when it works, it works really well.

Implementing the three tools discussed in this chapter will help you keep your love alive and allow it to grow, as you and your partner continue to evolve in your relationship. For love to work, you have to believe in it. I know many couples on second and third marriages who say they are happier than they have ever been. If you've had a false start or two, the truth is that you must have learned something in the process, and chances are you won't make the same mistakes again.

Being in love for life doesn't mean that you will stay with your high-school sweetheart. It means that at any time you can make the choice to change your situation and make your life one of love and support. You won't always be right, and your mate won't always laugh at your jokes, but if you work to create true love, you will have something more precious than diamonds. Ask anyone who has lost the love of their life what they would trade to have that person back. Make the most of what you have. It is a gift.

Conclusion

Creating positive habits as a couple will ensure that you have a good relationship. Reading this book and doing the exercises is an expression of caring and desire, and it will help to delineate and refine each of your roles. As a couple, you want to know what to expect from each other, and hopefully the two of you have developed some new habits (or you've refined those you already had) that will help you understand and get along with each other much better.

Knowing what to expect creates a sense of security, which is often absent in the ordinary functioning of relationships. You can even share your expectations with family and friends, who will want to know where to find help when something goes wrong in their relationships. Expanding on this idea, communicating about how to solve problems before they become bigger problems leads to a greater level of mutual respect. This book has given you many useful communication tools.

Making a mutual commitment to improve your habits with your partner will have a positive influence on the quality of all your relationships. People simply do better when they know who cares about them and what they are willing to do for one another.

It would be nice to live in a perfect world, but we don't. Bad things still happen. We can't control events, but we can control how we respond to them. This is another reason why creating good habits as a couple is so important. Being in a strong relationship with a loving partner will help you face whatever comes along.

If you have worked your way through this book, you have done well. This doesn't mean that you're done, or that you should ever stop working on your relationship (reread chapter 24). It does mean that you may be able to work less hard in the future, because you have put your time and energy into making your relationship more positive and, I hope, more enjoyable. To help you make lasting changes, I've included a final list of the top ten ways to improve your relationship habits. Take this list with you, and use these and all of your new or improved habits to make your relationship the best it can be.

Top Ten Ways to Improve Your Habits

1. **Become more aware.** Whether you figured the problem out on your own or it was pointed out to you, becoming aware that you inadvertently hurt someone will help you change your action from a negative to a positive.

2. **Remember to apologize.** A simple "I'm sorry" should be followed up with the question "What can I do to make up for it?" The answer you receive will move you to take helping and healing actions. And make sure not to repeat your mistakes.

3. **Think before you speak.** Before you speak, say to yourself what you want to tell your partner, and imagine how your partner will interpret what you say. If you imagine a negative reaction, you now have the opportunity to change your language for the better.

4. **Show empathy.** Put yourself in your loved one's shoes and feel what she is feeling. Empathizing with someone you care for can improve your own mood and help both of you feel better.

5. **Keep your temper.** Remember, when you fly off the handle, you usually will regret it. Try counting to ten before losing your cool. It's an old trick, but it works.

6. **Practice, practice, practice.** It takes about thirty repetitions to create a new habit. Keep integrating positive habits into your lifestyle and replace any bad habits with good ones.

7. **Listen when others speak.** Your partner may be your best guide when it comes to helping you recognize certain ways you could improve. Your partner is the one who is going to see (and be most affected by) your habits. Let the one you love help you make the changes that will leave both of you happier.

8. **Remember that relationships have to be win-win.** When you're in a relationship, if one of you loses, both of you do. Trying to win an argument is only going to cause more hurt. If you can't fix it so that both of you feel like winners, put the issue away for a while and look at it again later.

9. **Believe in yourself.** You have the ability to change and even improve your habits. It does take determination and discipline, but if you start small, making larger changes will become much easier with time and experience.

10. **Remind yourself that you want this.** Your desire to be a better person may be your most powerful ally when it comes to making positive changes. People change and get better every day, and you can too. All you have to do is decide that you want to be one of them.

At some point in our lives, we all must confront our bad habits. When it comes to the habits that we manifest in our relationships, confronting them can be more challenging, but it's worth it.

It's time to confront your own bad habits and turn them around. You can do it. The process will probably not be as difficult as you imagine, and the rewards can be great. So go for it. I promise you'll be happy you did.

Barton Goldsmith, PhD, is a multi-award winning psychotherapist, a syndicated columnist and radio host, and a recognized keynote speaker. He has appeared on many television shows and is frequently interviewed by the national press. He was named by *Cosmopolitan* magazine as one of America's top therapists, and is the author of a number of books, including *Emotional Fitness for Couples* and *Emotional Fitness for Intimacy*.

Foreword writer **Harville Hendrix, PhD**, is co-creator of Imago relationship therapy, and is known internationally for his work with couples. Hendrix is also the author of the *New York Times* bestsellers *Getting the Love You Want* and *Keeping the Love You Find*.